The
Bible Bluff

ISBN 978-1491217184 (sc)
ISBN 978-91-978399-3-8 (pdf ebook)
Also available on Kindle

First printed in Swedish 2005

Support with translation and publishing: Aaron Rose, USA

Other books in English by Mariana Stjerna:
Agartha – The Earth's Inner World (2013)
On Angels' Wings (2013)
Mission Space (2013)

SoulLink Publisher
www.SoulLink.se
info@SoulLink.se

Mariana Stjerna

The Bible Bluff

Jesus and Mary Magdalene

From Another Perspective

SoulLink Publisher

Jan Fridegård (1897-1968) grew up as a farm laborer and tried several professions before the debut of his writings: *One Night in July* (1933). His autobiographical novel trilogy about Lars Hård is perhaps his finest work. The death of his father aroused a latent interest in the supernatural, which came to be reflected in *The Tower Rooster* (1941).

Contents

Foreword

Many years ago my husband and I visited Glastonbury in England. It was in the month of May, when all England blossomed with a rare splendor. I was curious about the Grail story, which has always lain secretly dormant in my heart. Now I wanted to know more about it.

"The Tor"

Excavations have shown a complete spiral maze around the Tor. It is evidence of the hill's ritual use in Neolithic times, 6000–1800 BC.

A small path with steps led up to the world-famous well under which it is said that the Grail is hidden. When we reached the top we had a wonderful view over the lovely landscape, but the most interesting thing was Chalice Well, the well of the Grail. The source of the water of the well is unknown, but the water fills the five-sided well-chamber and flows through a separate pipe, from the spring underneath the garden, out through a lion's head. Even during severe drought the water never stops flowing. The well has a very beautiful wooden lid, and from here the water runs step by step down into the valley.

Chalice Well

The wooden lid above what is called the well of the Druids shows a pre-Christian symbol, which the early Christians believed to represent the sign of the Fish. It also represents the blending of the masculine and feminine and denotes the meeting-place of conscious and unconscious worlds.

When we visited this wonderful place we met an elderly lady tending the flowers. She looked as if she were straight out of an English gardening book from the eighteenth century. She wore a wide-brimmed straw hat and thin gloves and carried a basket on her arm. She had a clear-cut, friendly face, and she asked us if we were tourists.

Of course I asked her about the Grail. I told her that I had read somewhere that it was hidden near the well or maybe beneath it. She smiled and told us that she had seen the Grail – the real one! It really existed here in Glastonbury. It had been found and hidden again and was a very beautiful goblet with jewels and carvings. We had a long and interesting talk, but I am unfortunately unable to recall the details. She seemed very well informed about the history of Glastonbury. After that we wandered about in the surroundings of this magic well. We saw the beautiful thorn tree where Joseph of Arimathea is said to have planted his staff. He placed his staff into the ground of Wearyall Hill, and in that spot a hawthorn tree grew and flowered. We could not have seen the same one, but we may have seen an offshoot.

Many symbols are related to the Grail. Some sources tell us it is not a goblet, some say it never existed, Dan Brown believes it is a woman's (Mary Magdalene's) womb. Various artists have expressed very different ideas about the magic goblet and made it historic. I believe that the tale of the Holy Grail in this book is trustworthy. However, I ask the reader to form his or her own opinion.

A luxuriant offshoot of the thorn-tree that
Joseph of Arimathea planted with his staff.

Introduction

Ever since my confirmation I have had difficulties understanding and enjoying the Bible. I find it a very illogical book. I have tried talking to clergymen, but they seem to swallow everything without question. I have read the Apocrypha and a lot of gospels, besides the four in the Bible. I read about the Meeting of Bishops in Nicaea and was angry to see Christianity being treated in such a careless and arbitrary way – a religion they were supposed to be preaching.

From childhood I could not understand why anybody should be put on a pedestal. Are royalty, politicians, actors, or other celebrities more remarkable than you and me? As a child I thought, "Oh dear, they all need to go to the toilet!" Nobody can live forever, and that's something we all have in common. Of course there are different degrees of knowledge and wisdom, but that doesn't prevent people from being people. And that is what I want to relate: the human element in all the greatness and holiness described in the New Testament and, as far as that goes, in the whole Bible. The human element is the main theme in my search for the one and only Truth.

Jesus was searching for the Truth like you and me. He had supernatural powers because there are such powers. Some of us are born with them. If you seek them, you find them. He looked for them and found them on his journeys. But he also had a wife and two children, and he loved his family. I read somewhere that he found fasting unnecessary. You've got a body in order to care for it, not to make it consciously suffer, he thought.

If you feel shocked, hurt, or even offended by Jan's visits to the biblical story, please put this book away! But let me also explain that it acts as an intermediary of Love to the Truth and Beauty of what really happened. "The Truth shall set you free," said Jesus. But we don't always want the Truth, because we like to create our own Truth. After that we put on our blinders.

Come with me on a very unusual journey. Try to feel liberation instead of dismay. It is time that the Truth inside and outside people is revealed the way it was mediated to those who wanted to listen. This book is written in the I-form, because I will now deliver the words of my Angelic friend Jan.

Please, my dear readers, listen above all to your own Truth that is hidden in your heart.

– Mariana Stjerna

Message from an Angel

My name is Jan Fridegård. I want to introduce myself to you in order to explain how and why this book was written.

When I lived on Earth in my last incarnation I was quite a famous Swedish writer. My father was a farm worker. We were very poor, and I had a tough childhood. I wrote about my youth and people liked it and suddenly, after much hard work, I became popular. Before I died I told a friend that I had no intention to stop writing "up there." I found a medium (a psychic), Mariana Stjerna, and I am now able to tell you about my adventures in other worlds.

I now belong to the Angelic Realm. I have been here since 1968 and I have enjoyed every minute of it (although minutes don't exist here!). In two previous books I have described my journeys in the cosmos. In this book I made excursions into the times of the New Testament, and it was a thrilling experience. You may not recognize the names of my friends and companions, so here is some background information.

The Master Melchizedek is quite well-known, and can be found in the Bible. He belongs to what is called "The Great White Brotherhood" and he is a wonderful, humble man, a beautiful Spirit. I met him in my first struggle to be a nice Angel. (I like joking and jesting, and from time to time I can be a bit cheeky.)

Oshio was my leader on a planet where the Central Race lives. (You can read about the Central Race and the Wingmakers on www. wingmakers.com.) I was living there (as an Angel) when I was ordered to go back to the Angelic Realm and write this book.

Kualli is a kind of General for the Angelic "army." He was a Native American when he lived on Earth, and a very good leader of his tribe. He now organizes my travels between the worlds. He is a very interesting and wonderful spirit.

Zar is my best friend and companion among the Angels. He is one of the Masters and often follows me on my journeys. He and Kualli support my search for the Truth, and nothing but the Truth.

And now, dear readers, this journey into the past can begin!

1. Journey Home from the Central Race

Hello, Earth! This is the Truth-finder Jan from the Angelic Realm calling his medium on Earth. I have a lot to tell you. I have made the most fantastic journeys back in time, to biblical times. I wanted to know what really happened, and I did find out, sometimes in a very dramatic way. When I was called to make these journeys I was living in another reality, visiting the Central Race in another Universe. The Master who was leading my path was Melchizedek, and I was going to meet him again.

Melchizedek was waiting for me in the main library inside the great Cathedral. Of the High Masters, he is the one that I like the most. He is grand, strong, handsome, and full of warmth and humor. The main library is the beautiful room where we met Oshio the first time we visited the Central Race. Oshio is one of the cosmic guides and, to my great surprise, he came right towards me when I entered the Cathedral. When we had greeted, he took my hand and led me to the main library. I didn't dare to ask what would happen, but probably I would get a new mission. Melchizedek was standing at a large table with remarkable sculptured table legs. He embraced me and kissed my cheeks. Then we all three sat down on a comfortable sofa at the short side of the room.

"Dear Jan," the Great Master started, and I shivered with both excitement and curiosity. "I have called you here today because of your longing," he said, and observed me carefully at the same time as he grinned a friendly smile. "Don't you think we know that you long to go back to the Angels? You have completed the work tasks you have received here to our satisfaction. I have nothing to blame you for; I just want to reward you. We plan to send you back to the Angelic Realm. Kualli and I have decided this, since you have new tasks waiting for you there, and your group needs you. What do you say about that?"

"When may I go?" I asked, and probably my eyes were shining. Think about returning home again! I would get closer to my beloved Earth. That alone was wonderful.

"Soon," Melchizedek promised and exchanged a look of mutual agreement with Kualli. My interior cheered. They wanted me back over there. I would become myself again! At least I felt so.

I have no memory of the journey back to the Angelic Realm, and perhaps I wasn't supposed to have that either. What is termed magic on Earth is an everyday occurrence on this level. When I awoke I felt soft down feathers under my back and I immediately glided down a familiar slide, consisting of the wing of the Angel Jolith.

My friend Oshio had disappeared and so had Melchizedek. Instead I flew into the familiar arms of Zar, a dear friend and leader. I knew very well the flourishing meadow we had landed on. Behind Zar my Angelic group was singing out loud and threw flowers at me. I felt very welcomed indeed.

"You need to rest for a while," said Zar, and he took me to my own dwelling, which stood in beautiful surroundings just as I had left it. I don't know how long I had been in the promised land of the Central Race. Time means nothing here, and I would soon learn that in a more tangible way. It was nice to be back home, and I instantly laid down on my bed and fell asleep – for how long, I don't know.

Zar woke me up. "You've had your sleep, and you are now ready for your new tasks," he said, smiling. "We need you for a great and thrilling mission. I think you will like it, because it will be an adventure, and yet, at the same time, you will stay in the Angelic Realm. You will have your base here."

Now my curiosity had been awakened, and as I prepared for the upcoming visit with General Kualli, I bombarded Zar with questions. He just smiled and refused to answer. I had to wait; he was not going to present the mission to me, Kualli was. He was certainly the highest General of the Angelic Army, and he was a tremendously wise and interesting person and in addition to that an Indian. So there was another happy reunion.

Kualli's room was comfortably and snugly decorated. Zar and I sat down on his lovely green silk sofa. Neither we nor the sofa were physical, so our weight on the sofa was invisible. I love putting my buttocks on a comfortable sofa without leaving any imprint!

"It's time for a fantastic revelation," began the General. I leaned forward and was all ears.

2. The Mission

"Our Mother Earth is not at all well," Kualli continued. "Humanity is living a lie, and this lie has repercussions for all people on Earth. It's time to expose that lie and that's what we are going to do in this book, but it will take some time for many people to accept what we are going to tell them. We will find the Truth by removing the curtain that hides the secrets of the origin and reveals what really happened. The secrets have been hidden for more than two thousand years. Now they shall be disclosed. 'The Truth shall set you free,' Jesus said. I say it depends on people's acceptance of the Truth."

"I don't understand anything," I said, looking deep into Kualli's eyes. His eyes were dark, almost black, with a golden spot shining near the pupil. His black hair reached to his shoulders and his face had an enigmatic, noble beauty that is quite common among Native Americans. The light brown color of his face made a beautiful contrast with his lilac-colored cloak. "Shall I change what is written in the Bible?" I continued. "I don't know if I want to. That old book has caused enough trouble in the world without our intrusion from here."

"Don't take it literally, Jan." Kualli smiled, and I noticed how much Zar was enjoying this conversation. "It's a matter of words for you to mediate through your medium on Earth. There will be plain speaking."

"Poor Mariana," I sighed. "She will be the scapegoat."

"I think she will be honored," Zar asserted. "Wait until you know what it is about."

"The Old Testament is a Jewish tale, built on real events in history, some chronicles, and some myths and legends," Kualli continued calmly.

"This, together with the New Testament, has been woven into an imposing epic, written by skillful men, mostly monks. Behind the epic, in the beginning, was a powerful man: the Roman Emperor

Constantine the Great (AD 272–337). His will is the feet of clay that the whole Bible colossus is resting on. Power and imagination are constant themes.

"Constantine was a strange and contradictive ruler. He was not a Christian, but he liked order and method and he admired the organization of Christianity. That is what he wanted for himself and that is why he encouraged the priests. He wasn't christened until his death-bed. And now listen to something important: Constantine summoned a church meeting in the year AD 325, in the little town of Nicaea, in Bithynia (current Turkey). More than 300 bishops came to that meeting, as well as a large number of spiritually interested and active persons. It took them two months to come to an agreement about what is now called the Nicene Creed."

"Kualli, my friend, is this a history lesson?" I joked. "I know very well that the Bible is our religious record. I was never interested in the Bible because it was shoved down my throat when I was a little child."

"No, Jan, this is no history lesson, just a reminder. We want you to understand the very basis of your mission." Kualli was very serious now. "I just want to tell you that this meeting included many people, many arguments, and endless discussions about the content of the Bible, and that it went on for a very long time. Those who made notes of the original text were mostly monks, but also good storytellers. The Jews had the Old Testament written down, but there was also a verbal tradition for centuries. The New Testament is a mixture of four gospels and some other tales. These gospels consist of a selection, made at the Meeting of Bishops. In fact, there were about eighty gospels to choose from, and they had to limit the contents of the Bible. There is much more to tell you about all of this, about the search that did not give priority to the Truth, but instead was focused to give the priesthood more power over the people.

"The Truth is not to be found in the four well-known gospels, but in some others, written during the time of Jesus and shortly afterwards. Most of them are not yet found – I'm referring to the present time on Earth. Most people on Earth are living a lie. They are cheated, totally betrayed. Perhaps the priests of today believe in what they preach, but they don't know how blind their faith is! Of course, there are good things in your Bible too, Constantine and the bishops saw to that. But when it comes to Jesus, both the Bible and all kinds of scientific research during the time that have elapsed since it was written have gone astray and facts have been horribly mixed up."

"But wasn't Jesus a Master and the Son of God?" I interrupted, rather frightened.

"Oh yes, he was a masterful prophet," Kualli smiled. "And he was God's Son in the same sense that all men and women are God's sons and daughters. Every human being carries a part of God inside them, but they use it to a greater or lesser extent. Jesus tried to tell about this; he didn't put himself in a unique position as God's favorite or his only Son. Other people did that. As he actually died almost 150 years before the Meeting of Bishops in Nicaea, and the Crucifixion took place 300 years before that Meeting, the priests could make rules for obedience, reverence, and absolute devotion to the religion that they had created. They were also able to erase certain important things, as you will soon understand. For two thousand years the priesthood has succeeded in pulling the wool over people's eyes and plugging their ears. Now we come to you, Jan!"

"Me!" I screamed, terrified. "What can I do about the faith of people or, even less, about the religions on Earth?"

"You can tell the Truth," Kualli replied calmly. "Of course you cannot do more than that. But you have to thoroughly know the Truth in order to tell it. We have planned a journey for you. This time you will be able to travel to various epochs in Earth's history and examine the original scriptures and events that are hidden there. You will be travelling outside your Angelic body, Jan! You will be able to materialize in different countries: biblical countries and some others. You will experience the undiluted gospels and some of the persons who have written them. You will experience yourself as an 'ordinary' human being for as long as you stay at a place, but at the same time you will know about your mission."

"So I will go to various ages in places that are connected with Christianity?" I asked, rather surprised.

"That is correct. We want you to find out the Truth by being present at secret events that your Bible didn't want to (or couldn't) report."

"Shall I investigate people in both the Old and the New Testament?"

"At the time we do not care about the Old Testament; that's a story that belongs to the Jews."

3. The First Shock: There Were Two Jesuses!

"There is one Truth," said Kualli, "that you must take with you on your trip, and that Truth is very important. Listen, Jan: There was not only one Jesus. Two prophets by the name of Jesus lived in the first century."

I stared at my old friend Kualli and my best friend Zar. Both were silent, staring intensely at me.

"Two Jesuses!" I shouted, "Two of them! That is crazy. Tell me you're joking! It's rather impudent to make such a joke, because two equal prophets couldn't have existed at the same time."

"Not equal," Zar answered. "The name Jesus was quite common at the time. The second Jesus was born when the first Jesus was already an adolescent, but their lives have been mixed up in many ways. You will have to find out the Truth."

I felt hesitant. Two prophets with the same name could certainly give rise to confusion and mix-up. If this was the case, there must be huge changes in the interpretations of the Bible. I suddenly felt like a pioneer, and I liked the feeling.

"There's a need for it," I said at last. "I will take the matter in hand. It sounds like a very exciting project. Can I meet both Jesuses?"

"Oh yes, you will," Kualli promised. "Your Bible version covering parts of the New Testament will overthrow most opinions. You are right, there's a need for it. It cannot go on like this. Constant fighting, battles, wars, violence, and common evil – all in the name of God and Christ."

"Why?" I asked. "Why has nobody found this out earlier?"

"They have," Kualli answered. "But who wants to throw away two thousand years of faith in the only Son of God? That is what we believe you are going to do. You are down-to-earth, skeptical, and curious enough to find out the Truth. We couldn't imagine anyone more suited to this task than you."

I felt both flattered, exuberant, and scared. It was child's play to travel to various indigenous tribes in other realities, compared to this mission. Partly I must have substantial knowledge, partly I had to know where I was aiming. I also had to know how it would happen.

Perhaps my old friend Zar divined the thoughts inside my frowning Angelic brow, because he softly put his hand on mine. "Don't worry, we will make the practical arrangements," he assured me. "The knowledge you have of the Bible is enough; the rest is up to us to manage. You don't need much knowledge at the outset, but on the other hand, you will acquire a great deal."

"But two Jesuses," I protested, "both in Jerusalem. Is that right?"

Kualli and Zar nodded. "They weren't active at the same time," said Kualli. "The second Jesus was about twelve years younger than the first one. Numbering them sounds too blasphemous. Let us call the first one Jesus and the second one Issa, making it more comprehensible. Issa is the name of the younger Jesus when he lived in exile in Kashmir."

"Was he also persecuted?" I asked. "He wasn't crucified, was he?"

"No, but he had to escape from Palestine because people confused them and the first Jesus was persecuted. Issa really suffered for what Jesus did, but he didn't see it in that light. He was a very intelligent and wise man and a very skilled healer."

"How can I get there?" I asked. "How do I dive into a prehistoric age? How is it reached?"

"Time doesn't exist," answered Kualli calmly. "You know that. All time on Earth before Now is preserved as a kind of imprint in the Universe. If you like, you can call it holograms. We will send you to the various places while your Angelic body sleeps here. It may seem like a dream to you, although you will be completely conscious about what you see and hear, and you will experience yourself as physical. It is nothing like hypnosis. It is our own invention. We will talk after each 'dream.' I am sure there will be much to discus."

"Come on, then!" I was enthusiastic. "It will be great fun."

Zar took me to another room in the Angelic school. There was a comfortable bed, a couple of armchairs, and a table with a recording-machine on it. I lay down on the bed. After a short while, a woman came into the room. She must be an Angel, of course, I thought. She had a pleasant – in fact quite lovely – face and long, curly light brown hair, big blue eyes, and a finely chiseled profile.

"I will be your companion and leader on these travels," she said, putting her hand on mine. "My name is Lydia and I will be at your side, but mostly invisible."

"I have no objection to you being visible." I smiled, looking at her. She smiled back and disappeared.

"She is a religious historian," Zar explained. "She is very competent and very interested in the kind of events you are going to investigate. She will ensure that you are okay and she will be there to help you if you get into trouble. We do know you, Jan, and we know that adventures always have a way of catching up with you. You cannot and you may not change any historical event, even if you find yourself a part of it. Okay, let's begin. Lie down on your bed."

I did so, and Zar covered me with a sheet. I don't know what magic he worked, but I fell asleep immediately.

4. Rolls of Parchment, Not Yet Discovered

When I looked down at my body I wore a snuff-brown robe and on my naked feet I wore sandals. I looked around and saw that there was nothing but desert. Well, not entirely, since further away there were some gray rocks flocked around a big cliff.

"Are you there, Lydia?" I hissed. She soon appeared, the beautiful smiling lady I'd met a while ago.

"You can be assured that I am always here, at your side," she said quietly. "But please, don't call upon me unnecessarily. I will appear whenever I feel you need me."

I decided to walk to the cliffs. Not that I was used to walking in desert sand dressed in Arabic clothes, but it was surprisingly easy, although I had acquired human form. Soon I was facing a cave-like opening in the gray granite rock. A young boy crept backwards from the narrow entrance of the cave and ended up right in front of me. He was dressed in a loose shirt that was dirty and torn. He looked terrified when he saw me. He held several parchment rolls in his arms.

"I found them here," he cried, and to my surprise I could understand him. "I didn't steal them. They were inside the cave in an old earthen vessel with a lid. I thought I'd give them to our wise village chief. Who are you, stranger?"

"I'm from another village and I can read," I answered. He would probably be scared if I told him I was a stranger from another time. "I would like to have a look at those scrolls," I said.

He threw the scrolls in front of me and ran away. Terrified, he looked at something beside me. I turned around and Lydia was standing there, laughing.

"I had to appear for the boy," she said. "Otherwise he would not have given us the scrolls, and I feel we need to have a look at them."

"They couldn't be the Dead Sea Scrolls, could they?" I wondered, with awe in my stomach and knees. In front of me were very old parchments, yellow-brown and frayed. I would probably not be able to read them, but I carefully took one and rolled it out on the sand. The writing seemed well-preserved, plainly written in a clear hand.

"No, they're not the Dead Sea Scrolls," Lydia assured me with a smile. "Certainly the Dead Sea Scrolls were found in this desert, but these seem to be older. I think you were led here just because these scrolls have remained undiscovered until this day."

"But the Arab boy found them," I objected irritably. "It seems like it must be either the Dead Sea Scrolls or the other ones that were found near Qumran."

"Here there are many rocks and many caves," my lovely companion continued. I could still see her, and she seemed very physical. "Do you believe that all boys in dirty shirts find Dead Sea Scrolls in caves?"

"No," I answered, a little embarrassed. "Are we not in a desert now?"

"We are on a tableland," Lydia said. "Look around you more carefully!"

I realized I had only looked one way. I was standing on sand, but all around me as far as I could see there were small rocks and high hills. The vegetation was sparse, but bushes and grass were everywhere.

"You are in a wasteland near the place where the Qumran monastery was located," continued Lydia. "Perhaps the author of the scrolls, himself, put them into the cave. You can see that the opening of the cave is very low, and no one but a very thin person or a child could wriggle past it. These scrolls haven't been found yet, Jan, not even in your modern times (the twenty-first century). They are waiting for their discoverer. We wanted to show you their repository, and now we want to show you when they were written. After that we have to put them back here, because they are history."

"Why am I dressed in an Arabian burnous, and what will happen to the boy? Are there more scrolls in the cave?" I really felt confused.

"Oh Jan, you are not dressed in a burnous! Can't you tell Arabian clothes from a simple monk's habit?" Lydia laughed. "The boy will come back with men from his tribe, and we shouldn't still be here then. Yes, there are more scrolls in there, but these are enough for us. We have the beginning of our story in these scrolls, and you will get the next part from the author himself. But you have to read these first. They contain the shocking Truth about the second Jesus, the second prophet."

"Who will decipher them?" I wondered. Lydia motioned for me to pick them up. I got an armful. At this juncture, we heard shouts and screams. Far away we saw a trail of men, armed with cudgels and swords glinting in the sun. Lydia took my hand and we both disappeared – with the scrolls. I don't know how it happened, but I opened my eyes in the room where the dream had started. Was it a dream? Do Angels dream?

"It was no dream, dear Jan," said Kualli, taking my hand. "You and Lydia managed this very well. Thank you for the scrolls; they shall immediately be deciphered so we can read them. Their contents will lead us further. You must get used to the monk's habit; it's very useful in many situations. I believe that soon we will have some interesting reading and guidance for our next step."

On one of the walls in the room, text appeared. It looked like subtitles on a movie screen. What it said startled me once again at the ignorance of people – or the fact that, for ages, they have been kept ignorant of the Truth. The language of the scrolls was very old-fashioned and complicated, but I will try to translate it into a more modern language.

5. An Unknown Gospel

It is now fifty years after the Crucifixion of our beloved Master Jesus Christos. I, Simon Zebedee, describe a remarkable human fate, which is closely associated with the life of the Master. As a scribe and a close friend of Joseph of Arimathea, I assure the reader of my scroll that what is written here is the unconditional Truth. I am an old man now, but my memory is unsullied and reliable. In the course of time I made notes and they have helped me to write this scroll. I will tell you about the younger Jesus (Issa) who was also a very great prophet, but not in the country of his birth. He was like a son to me.

Jesus (Issa) was born in Jerusalem at the same time that the older Jesus was in Jerusalem with his parents. At that time, Jesus was twelve years old. As was customary with boys at that age, he visited the Temple of Jerusalem at the Passover festival in order to be examined by the board of the elders. At the same time, in a beautiful house in the middle of the town, a young woman called Mary (like the mother of Jesus) was in labor pains. Her husband was a merchant and a Nazarean, and thus he didn't belong to the Jewish belief. The Nazareans were the original Christians, and they were not in favor with the Jews.

The merchant Judas Immanuel was highly esteemed by most people in Jerusalem. He led an honorable life with his wife Mary and four daughters. Mary wished for a son this time, and her wish was fulfilled. There was nothing strange or supernatural about the birth of this little boy. There were no Angels singing, but the child smiled almost at once and he seemed to recognize his parents. Jesus was a common name at that time and the boy was baptized Jesus Ibrahim because his mother wished him to have that name. Her father and her beloved brother were both called Ibrahim.

At the time of his baptism in the temple, a sunbeam fell right on top of the head of the child and stayed there during the whole ceremony. It was considered peculiar and unusual, and the young Mary was convinced that her son was going to be a great prophet. His father was of a different opinion. As Jesus (Issa) was the only son, his father expected him to be an heir to his well-established company.

Jesus (Issa) grew up to be a wise and beautiful boy. He loved animals very much, and the family's home soon was filled with different animals found by the boy in nature. They were often half dead or wounded. He cured them. His father thought that the boy's common sense and patience cured the animals, but his mother considered her son a chosen one from the Angelic hierarchy showing his divine heritage for the humans. He had the gift of healing, and that gift was considered to be given to him through the sunbeam at his baptism. His sisters were not at all impressed and treated him as a spoiled child.

In the beginning no one but his parents, sisters, and some friends knew about his gift of healing. To boast about this could annoy the Jews and provoke them into calling him a traitor. I was the only one who knew about this, because I was a friend of his father. I also often talked to Joseph of Arimathea, and that way I could compare the talents of both boys. I knew that the older Jesus was wandering about in Palestine and also in other countries. I had heard some of his prophecies and speeches and I had also witnessed some of his miracles. When I told Joseph about the younger Jesus, who had grown up to a young man in his early twenties when the older Jesus was crucified, he didn't want to listen. For him, there was only one Jesus of importance.

I was of a different opinion. The young Jesus had not yet a reputation as a prophet, but he performed miracles among the small circle of people who surrounded him. After the Crucifixion of Jesus Christos, I joined that circle. I was curious to know how Jesus Ibrahim lived and taught. His father was deeply worried. His son didn't want to work as a merchant, in spite of the prosperous business. His father was involved with the Essenes, a brotherhood living in villages on the other side of Jordan. Among other things, he sold their textiles, specimens of woodwork, dried herbs, and also some fresh food. I knew that the young prophet had acquired a lot of their knowledge and faith and that he tried to spread these among his friends. But that, too, was dangerous, since the Romans hunted the Essenes.

Here I had to interrupt. "Kualli, I don't know much about the Essenes," I confessed, feeling rather embarrassed. "It will be easier for me when I read the scroll if I know who they are. Was it a cult or a religion?"

"Neither," Kualli said, smiling. "They were simply a brotherhood that dated back to unknown times – in any case, very long ago. According to old scriptures, Christianity came with the Essenes and not with Jesus. He preached what he had learned in Essene monasteries and on his journeys. Something quite different was fabricated in the year AD 325, at the Meeting of Bishops in Nicaea. But I will give you a swift history of the Essenes, because I think we will hear more about them in connection with the two Jesuses.

"You would know a lot more about the Essenes if you had read the Dead Sea Scrolls. A group of them lived in the monastery of Qumran, another in the monastery at Mount Carmel. They also lived in other places in Palestine and in Egypt, near to the water. Many of their villages and monasteries were situated at the river Jordan. In their villages there were good craftsmen, gardeners, farmers, smiths, carpenters, tanners, and others. The villages were in fact like big families. Today you would call them communes. The family was revered and the children were important, both one's own children and others'.

"The Essenes took care of orphans and abandoned children. They lived very healthy and most of them were vegetarians. The women helped each other to spin, weave, sew, and cook. In the monastery there were only men. They used to rise at sunrise, go down to the shore, and bathe. They were always in contact with the four elements, and the forces of nature were holy to them. After bathing they dressed in clean white cloaks, woven in one piece, and meditated together.

"When they worked they all shifted to simple gray cloaks. This applied both to the monks in the monasteries and the men in the villages. But the most essential thing is that for many hundreds of years – yes, even for many thousands of years before Christ – the Essenes lived according to what we now call the principles of Christianity. Of course, no church would admit that, but you can read about it in the Dead Sea Scrolls and in many other scrolls both discovered and not yet discovered. You, yourself, will experience the Essenes, so I do not need to tell you more. The scroll continues."

All this seemed very exciting and I went on reading old Simon Zebedee's message about the two Jesuses.

Judas Immanuel, the father of Jesus (Issa), decided to send his son to Qumran. There he would get a very thorough education and at the same time learn reverence and respect. Jesus started at the school when he was ten years old and stayed there until he was twenty. These ten years of learning then characterized his whole life. Jesus Ibrahim grew into a knowledgeable and developed Essene. He was neither orthodox nor unfaithful; he was just an Essene.

The elders in Qumran wanted him to stay in the monastery as a teacher and researcher, but he wanted to build his own circle of disciples and pursue the knowledge he had already gained. There were possibilities for further education at Carmel, but first Jesus Ibrahim wanted to see more of the world. He had learned about other countries at Qumran – now he wanted to see them. He therefore went to Egypt. There he met several wise men, but also poor and sick people. He divided his time between wisdom and charity, which also included healing. He found the history of Egypt fascinating and he stayed there for longer than he had planned.

In the meantime, the Crucifixion of Jesus Christos took place in Jerusalem. Jesus Ibrahim knew nothing about it. What he knew about Jesus Christos he had learned in Qumran, and from what he had heard the first Jesus was some kind of god, only subordinate to the Great God and the Father. This Son of God or Messiah was high on his list and he decided to return to Jerusalem in order to find the prophet.

When Jesus (Issa) came back to Jerusalem, his old friends and disciples received him with great devotion. He showed me great veneration and often visited me. We would sit for hours in my house and talk about the strangest things. He was dismayed to hear that his highly admired Jesus Christos had died on the cross. Not even the closest friends knew that Christos' life was saved in the tomb of Joseph of Arimathea. I knew, because I was close to Joseph. But it was a secret that must be kept. The truth was that Jesus Christos was in the monastery at Carmel.

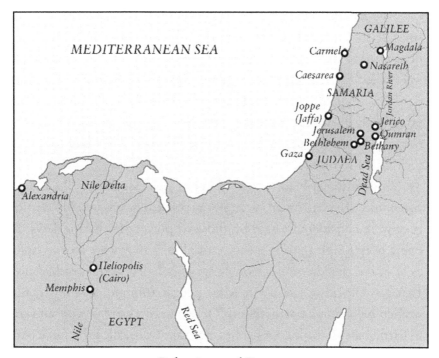

Palestine and Egypt

Jesus Ibrahim decided to follow in the footsteps of his predecessor. He thought that Palestine was his field of work, in the same way it was for Jesus Christos. He wandered around and preached a mixture of what he had learned at Qumran, on his long journey to Egypt, and his own experiences. But Jesus (Issa) was much more unobtrusive than his namesake. He knew how dangerous it could be to be a prophet. The Romans still hunted the Essenes and he suffered a lot because he didn't dare preach his beliefs everywhere.

"Kualli, I want to hear more about the religion of the Essenes," I interrupted. "I cannot understand how their teaching is supposed to be the first Christianity. Did Jesus Christos learn from them?"

"Oh yes, a lot," Kualli answered. "The Essenes lived in many places and they had schools in many monasteries, such as in Qumran and Carmel. Their seat of honor was Heliopolis in Egypt. They were very clever doctors, teachers, philosophers, scientists, poets, and artists. They were adepts in the art of living. Some of them reached far above the age of a hundred years.

"The Essenes were a brotherhood that existed in Palestine at the time of the birth of Jesus. Historical documents tell us that they descended from Greece, because the priests in the old Ephesus temple were called Essenes. The brotherhood existed long before Christianity, partly in Egypt and partly in Palestine, where the first monastery was established in Engedi, near the Dead Sea. Because of the jealousy of the priests and the despotism of those in power, they had to live in seclusion and silence.

"As mentioned before, the villages of the Essenes are like today's communes. The settlements were always situated near water. In Palestine they were considered a sect by those in power and by the Jews. In many holy scriptures, for instance the Bible, they were looked upon as heathens. Furthermore, women were included in the brotherhood. That was shocking, wasn't it? Most people thought so. How could women belong to a brotherhood? Of course, no women were allowed to participate in the higher studies, but they were called the Associates. In that context, it must be mentioned that the Essene women really performed humanitarian work. They took care of orphans and brought them up as if they were their own. There was a peaceful and loving co-operation among the inhabitants of the villages.

"You asked me about their teaching. I will try to give an account of the most important facets of their faith, which also was their way of life.

"Early in the morning, the Essenes started to move forces that gave them energy for the whole day. They worked consciously with a way of thinking, letting the good thoughts of the early morning influence the whole day. Likewise, the last thought before going to sleep was also very important. That was the thought that affected the subconscious during the night. Because of that they contacted the Celestial Forces, with the Angels. Problems then could be solved during sleep, making sleep a creative source.

"Besides the way of thinking, the Essenes prioritized taking good care of their bodies. Food and cleanliness were very important. They always tried to create harmony between body and soul, i.e., physically and psychically. They had to be in harmony with the Natural Forces.

This is how the Essenes regarded the Earthly Forces:

- The Sun is a very important source of energy that one should enjoy.
- Water is an essential element of life.
- The energies of the air should be received through breathing.
- The diet should be right in order to provide balance in the organism.
- Man is responsible for his/her own development.
- Earth represents two aspects of the fertility force. One of the aspects creates life from the soil, the other is the sexual energies of man.
- Health is achieved through harmonious relationships with all the forces of Earth.
- Joy is one of the most important rights of man. The inner harmony is built up through the feeling of joy and the radiation of joy.

The Essenes expressed the Cosmic Forces in the following way:

- Power results in both co-operation and lack of co-operation with other powers and forces in accordance with the irrefutable law of cause and effect.
- Love is expressed through kindness to others and affects the individual's health.
- Wisdom means that man has learned to understand the cosmic order and his/her own role in the cosmos.
- Protection of values is the same as to preserve all that is useful. To destroy what is good, both physically and psychically, means that you co-operate with the negative.
- Creation is to use the creative powers, enabling them to serve the works of the Creator.
- Eternal life means sincerity in relationships and to revere the Nature forces and the forces in the cosmos.
- Work shall be performed with care and efficiency.
- Peace is to be created by every individual both within and outside himself/herself. The state of the human collective is dependent on the state of all its atoms and the individuals who have joined them together. The individual should feel the inner peace deep inside and try to spread it wherever he/she is.

"Are you pleased now, Jan?" asked Kualli with a smile.

"Well," I answered, "this is nothing new. I thought their teaching was epoch-making!"

"Isn't it?" Now he was really laughing. "If people lived by these rules the world would look quite different. These rules have existed for thousands of years in different versions but nobody cares about them, do they? Now I think we will go on with old Simon's story."

6. Jesus Ibrahim Becomes a Prophet

While the older Jesus, called Christos, was hiding with his friends, the Essene monks at Carmel, Jesus (Issa) was spending a lot of time pondering upon how he was to proclaim his teaching the best way. He visited several of the disciples of Christos, but they showed him total unresponsiveness. For them there was only one Messiah, incarnated as Jesus Christos. Nobody should try to take his place. Thomas was the only one who was kind and open-hearted to Jesus Ibrahim. They soon became very good friends.

Night after night, Jesus Ibrahim and I sat in my humble home, discussing various possibilities. I knew that Jesus Christos was in Carmel. Joseph of Arimathea told me about the pain the prophet felt when he had to send his beloved wife Mary Magdalene and their little son David to Gaul. She was pregnant again and would have been in great danger if she had stayed in Palestine. Their first son, David, might become a dangerous prophet like his father. The Romans don't like prophets, but the people love them. The Romans believe they are a dangerous factor of power. Our poor empire is consumed by the foolish will of the Roman Emperor. Our freedom has been chained fast by an abuse of power and autocracy. We are not a people any longer, we are just a field, where all the seeds have grown wild due to lack of consensus during sowing. The seeds are threatened by genocide. The Emperor is always there, ready to mow where he wants to mow.

Like the older Jesus, my friend Jesus Ibrahim assembled his faithful ones in the Garden of Gethsemane. They were singing and dancing in order not to be suspected by Roman spies. They pretended they were celebrating something suitable for all ears. But among all ears there might be some unwanted ears, which was the case here.

"I exist in the Wholeness and the Wholeness exists in me," said the young teacher. It was one of his favorite phrases. "The Wholeness exists in you, too. Look inside yourselves and you see the beginning and the end of the world.

If you don't give the world what it wants, you will not get back what you want from the world. The whole world, heaven and eternity, is to be found inside each one of you. You are kings and queens, holy ones, and gods, each one of you, if you just have the strength to look inside yourselves."

When the unwanted ear heard such words, the words were sent on to another unwanted ear, whose owner continued to pass it forward. Kings and queens, holy ones, and gods were very dangerous words. People who listened to these words could even believe them and imagine things.

The faithful ones overheard the danger. They warned Jesus Ibrahim not to teach in Gethsemane any more. He hid in my house while we were planning his escape. He had to get away from Palestine before he met the same fate as his predecessor. I talked to Joseph of Arimathea. Even though he didn't acknowledge "my" Jesus as a prophet, the rumor had reached him that another prophet posed a threat to the Roman Emperor. It was high time to leave Palestine.

Jesus Ibrahim had found himself a wife. They were not yet married, only betrothed. She was the daughter of my neighbor, who worked in the vineyards. She was a beautiful girl, and she had the same name as the prophet's mother. She was also called Mary. Perhaps that explained why Jesus spent so much time at my place. The two youngsters often met in my simple house. Maria had the gift of listening, but also the gift of expressing herself. She could read and write. She was an unusual woman.

At last we agreed that the young couple should flee to Kashmir. I had heard a lot about Kashmir from Joseph of Arimathea, which in turn had heard Jesus Christos tell about it. First Jesus and Mary had to be wed secretly at one of my friends' place when they were on their way out of Palestine. All this was so urgent that we immediately started to make practical preparations for the journey. I declined to follow them, since I didn't want to leave my family in spite of my fatherly feelings for Jesus Ibrahim. But his mother, who was a widow, wanted to accompany them to Kashmir. We assumed that there would be a small caravan, because some friends also wanted to follow their prophet.

The journey started on a feasting day in Jerusalem. The Roman soldiers were out among the people in the middle of Jerusalem during these days.

We – Jesus, Mary, and I – had said farewell the previous day. My eyes were full of tears, and I held them both for a long time in my arms. I knew we were doing the right thing and that Jesus was born to be a prophet – but perhaps not the prophet of Jerusalem.

The caravan assembled in front of one of the gates of Jerusalem. We gave the guard a cup of wine with sleeping herbs in it, or else he would have asked us too many questions and maybe not allowed the caravan out. I followed them all the way to the gate. The caravan contained a lot of people with a lot of luggage. To my great surprise, Thomas was one of the travelers. He couldn't know that his beloved first Master was hiding in the monastery at Carmel. I followed the long trail of the caravan as it became smaller and smaller, as far as my eyes could gaze upon it. I knew that I would never see any of them again.

To finish this document, I want to tell you that in due course I got the news that Jesus Ibrahim had become a great prophet in Srinagar and its surroundings. His name was changed to Issa, or Yuza Asaf. It is said that the king, Gopanada, received him well – but that is only a hearsay which I have received from some travelling merchants.

I hope my dear friend Jesus Ibrahim from Jerusalem has received a dignified destiny. May his good and pure name forever be a holy and loving whisper in the eternal cosmos.

I, Simon, certify that this document tells the Truth and nothing but the Truth concerning my friend Jesus Ibrahim, the son of Judas Immanuel and his wife Mary.

"Well, what do you say now?" Kualli asked, with a tremble in his voice.

"I say that everything and nothing was as we thought it would be," I muttered. "But tell me about the journey. Did he and Mary have any children? How did he become a prophet in a foreign country?"

"That's what we would like you to find out, dear Jan," Kualli said, smiling. "Lie down on the bed again and then you will get out and travel."

7. A Shimmering Journey to Kashmir

"Now you have to wake up, Jan!" A woman's teasing voice woke me. Of course that voice came from the charming Lydia. Drowsily I sat up and looked around. I was sitting on the ground near a lake. On the lake there was something really intriguing: a lot of houses floating peacefully on the waves. I had never seen the like.

"Srinagar," Lydia declared. She was physical now, standing at my side. "It's the capital of Kashmir – if you don't know that already. We are going to find the second Jesus, the one who has become a prophet here."

"I thought we were going to visit Simon in Jerusalem, who wrote that document," I said, surprised.

"You wanted to know what happened to Issa here," objected Lydia. "When Simon wrote his document he was very old and did not know what happened to Jesus. So we had better walk into the time of the younger Jesus in Kashmir straight away."

I instantly crawled up. Now I was to meet the second Jesus. Hurray! But how could we find him?

"He is already rather well-known here under the name Issa," Lydia "answered" my thought. "Of course we will walk to his house now."

The house was situated in a flourishing garden. I was glad that it was not one of the water houses. This house was outside the town and overlooked the inner parts of the country. It was a pretty little house and I saw several people walking around inside. A couple of children played near a well. Lydia disappeared before anyone had noticed us. I missed her at once; it was much nicer with company in a foreign place like this.

I went up to a man who was sitting on the stairs outside the house. He had a rather long beard. When he got up I saw he was tall and lean. His brown hair with some white streaks reached to his shoulders. He had remarkable green-brown eyes that seemed to flash. He stretched his arms out to me and gave me a beautiful, welcoming smile, showing a dazzling white row of teeth.

"Brother," he said – and to my great surprise I understood him. No, I thought, I must stop being astonished. This isn't really happening, even if it seems that way. "Brother from far-away, I bid you welcome to my home. You will soon meet my wife Mary, who will offer us refreshments in this blessed heat."

I saw a woman coming out from the house with a jar and two cups. Although she was not that young any more, she was very beautiful. Her stomach was big and round, and I understood another child was on its way. A young girl and a somewhat younger boy followed her. The girl carried a plate with something that looked like cookies.

"Here you see my wife and my children, Miriam and Amin," he continued. "I knew you were coming, brother from far-away. Simon sent me the message."

"Simon!" I exclaimed. "But he is in Jerusalem!"

Jesus – because it must be him – shook his head. "Simon exists in another reality," he answered. "He is what you call dead, but he is very much alive in me and we still talk a lot with each other, more often now after his death than before."

"Are you Issa?" I asked.

He nodded. "Issa, or Yuza Asaf," he smiled, "or any other of all the names they give me. But if you ask me if I am Jesus Ibrahim, I also answer yes."

"You have stayed here with your family," I said thoughtfully. "Where is your mother?"

"She didn't survive the journey," was the sad answer. "She is buried in Taxila. It was such a long and laborious expedition.

"Miriam was born soon after we reached Srinagar. I am so happy that Mary made it. She is a wonderful wife and a real support to me. I have become a prophet, you see. I always wanted to be one and now I feel both honored and misunderstood. What's your name?"

"I'm called Jan. Why do you feel misunderstood?"

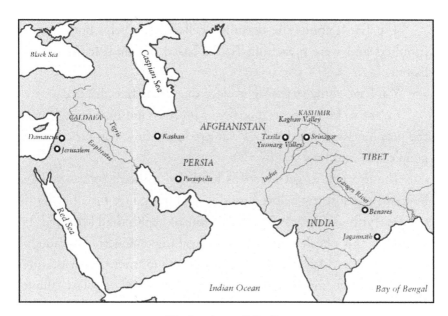

Kashmir and India

"At home in Palestine there wasn't room for two prophets called Jesus. I don't know if any prophet was welcome there. The prophets had to be eradicated in order to give the Romans absolute power. This may have changed now, but I don't return home. Many of my supporters followed me here. One of them is Thomas, who was also a disciple of Jesus Christos. Here he is."

A middle-aged man came wandering into the garden. He was of medium height, with sharp features and friendly brown eyes. His hair was black and a short beard covered his chin. He reached out his hand to me.

"Peace be with you," he said, smiling. This was the well-known Essene greeting that has remained in some places until today. "I'm Thomas, but here I'm called Ba'bat."

"Peace be also with you, brother," I answered. "I am Jan, and I come from another reality. I'm visiting the various realities where both Jesus-prophets reside, because I am a seeker of the Truth."

"There are many Truths," answered Thomas ambiguously. "Which one do you seek?"

"The Truth about the two men called Jesus, who both became prophets and were preaching Truths based on the teachings of the Essenes."

"You have come to the right place then," Thomas decided.

"I want to know more about your journey and how Jesus became the prophet Issa," I insisted. "I want to know how you preach to the people here and how you live."

"The journey to get here was hard and difficult," answered Issa hesitantly. "I lost my beloved mother and felt guilty for allowing her to come with us. She was in a worse state of health than I realized. I'm a prophet and a healer, but I couldn't heal my own flesh and blood. It was terrible, and I hesitated to continue the journey. She had gotten pneumonia that shortened her life. It all happened very fast. She fell ill when we came to Taxila, not far from the border of Kashmir. That's where she is buried. When I repented of bringing her with us, she was angry with me. The most important thing in her life had been giving birth to me, and she wanted to follow me until the end. She died in my arms. I was born from her body and her body died in my embrace."

"Somebody told me that the ten lost tribes of Israel were sent to the east, to Kashmir. Is that true?" I asked, and Issa smiled.

"Oh yes," he said. "We met them on our way here. They call themselves Bani Israel, which means the sons of Israel. Their number has increased, and today many of them live among the people here in Srinagar. They don't deny their origin."

"Do you know what Yuza Asaf means?" asked Thomas. I shook my head. "It means 'Leader of the healed lepers,' and I think that is why Issa has become so popular here. He has cured many lepers."

Issa dismissed this with a gesture. He did not like boasting.

"We then went on to Kashmir through the valley of Yusmarg," continued the prophet. "There we met the Yadu people, who are also remnants of the ten lost Israelite tribes."

"I've never heard of them," I sighed.

"The Yadu people earn their living by farming and cattle breeding, and they are well aware of their origins," Issa went on. "Their valley is on the same road that the merchants use, between Afghanistan and the Kaghan valley in Kashmir. But I know that our route is not the only thing you're interested in. I believe it's my destiny to preach the old wisdom to the people here. That task goes on and will not end with my death. After that someone else will continue. We have many followers, because the people of Kashmir love to listen to the words of God."

"Yes, Jan!" Thomas interrupted eagerly. "One day Raja Shalewahin was wandering on the mountain when he met Issa, who was fair-skinned and clad in white. The raja asked him his name and where he came from. Issa answered that he was born in a country far away, a country where people had forgotten the Truth and had succumbed to Evil. The king asked him to tell him about his religion and Issa answered that he taught people Love, Truth, and Purity of the heart and also to serve God, who dwells in the center of the Sun and the elements in an eternal and endless existence."

"Is that why time seems to stand still here?" I asked.

"Yes, stranger Jan, you're right," answered Issa. "Time stands still. That is when we must enter into it. If we can, we will meet the eternal Beingness."

8. In the Garden of Gethsemane

"You are talking about Christianity," I said. "But what does Christianity mean to you, and is it the same Christianity that your namesake preached?" I asked.

"Neither I nor Jesus Christos invented the name Christianity," answered Issa. "It came much later, long after our deaths. The Essenes are the source of much of the wisdom that the first Jesus and later I preached. Since my old friend Simon Zebedee taught me so much about the Essenes, this wisdom came to characterize everything I taught. Thomas has also helped me a lot with this. He is an Essene. Together we have travelled in this area, among other places to the monastery of Hemis. There we were received with open arms because my predecessor had been there. Our talks with the Buddhist monks were very interesting and profound. Do you know what conclusions we came to? We found out that the difference between our religions is minimal. True Christianity, as taught by the Essenes, and Buddhism both want humans to live the right way. There are lots of laws and other points of view where these two religions agree completely. But Jan, that is not what we are going to discuss now."

I didn't hear his last words; they became more and more diffuse. I had been called back home. My eyes tried to open, and the cool hand of Lydia was resting on my forehead.

"Oh dear, am I already back?" I complained. "It was so interesting to talk with Issa. I don't feel I have finished the conversation."

"You haven't finished it." Lydia smiled. "But now we know the most important things about Issa's journey from Jerusalem, about his family and about his preaching. We have met Thomas, and we will meet him again with Jesus Christos. Now we are going on a longer journey. So many important lies must be unveiled in order to reveal the Truth."

"Our Bible," I muttered, "The whole thing is a big Bible Bluff. People are cheated. But how can we make them understand that, when they have been living amid that lie for two thousand years?"

"Well, perhaps we can't," said Lydia softly, but then she continued in a sharper tone, "Two thousand years is the limit. Now it's really time to tell how things actually were."

"And if nobody believes in us?" I laughed. This was very amusing. I would have liked to have revealed it when I was an author on Earth. I delighted in thinking of all the people it would anger, not least the priests. Apparently I wasn't supposed to immerse myself in that kind of thought, because my consciousness totally disappeared.

The Garden of Gethsemane? Was this the way it looked? In any case that was the name an invisible Lydia whispered into my ear. I looked around and breathed an aromatic scent. The trees grew close together. There were cedars, olives, poplars, and many others I didn't recognize. It seemed to be a big herb garden. If you read about it in the Bible it seems to be a very small suburban garden, but now I could see that it stretched as far as the eye could view. There were cultivations everywhere. Flowers and herbs grew in small garden plots, framed by stones, that together created a pattern. It was really beautiful and soothing.

"We wanted you to meet Jesus Christos in his favorite surroundings," said Lydia, who apparently still had decided to remain invisible in this place.

I had no time to answer, because a man was coming towards me. He was not alone; a gathering of about twenty people followed him. I understood this was the "first" Jesus. He was fairly tall. His light brown hair and beard reminded me of all the paintings of him I had seen, but his face was different. What fascinated me the most was his eyes. They shifted in different colors: sometimes blue, sometimes green, and sometimes brown. That has to be an optical illusion, I thought. But while I was thinking, he was already standing near the tree where I was. He held the hand of a little boy, about two years old. At his side he had a beautiful woman with long, red-brown hair.

She showed signs of advanced pregnancy. They both smiled at me.

"Welcome to Gethsemane," said Jesus. He had a dark and sonorous voice. "I know who you are. You are the man who will escort my wife Mary Magdalene to safety in another country. What's your name?"

"I'm Jan," I answered, and gave him a trembling hand. He laughed, embraced me, and kissed both of my cheeks. Then he took Mary Magdalene's hand and put it into mine.

"Take care of all three of them for me," he requested. "The boat leaves from Joppe (current Jaffa) tomorrow evening if the wind is good. You can stay here for a while, so we can talk in peace and quiet. Thereafter your journey will begin after dark. This close to Jerusalem you would be regarded as fugitives if you meet someone who knows you. But when you have reached a couple of miles from here you're safer. Jan, you will play the part of a rich merchant, and you must pretend that my family is your family."

"I think you are mistaken, Master," I stammered. "I come from the future in order to find the Truth. Wouldn't Joseph of Arimathea be a better companion for Mary Magdalene?"

"Maybe he was somewhere else," Jesus said, smiling mysteriously. "Nonetheless, I entrust my wife, my son David, and my unborn child into your hands. I know that you will take them to a certain place in Gaul. Yes, my dear Jan, I want you to tell the Truth to posterity – the posterity that lies two thousand years into the future. In Gaul, a Jewish settlement is waiting for my wife and our children. There you will be taken care of."

"But … but," I stuttered, "the Jews are your real enemies, are they not? It is the Jews who will crucify you, Lord."

"Perhaps the history in your Bible does not fully conform with reality," he objected. "What is written there is a completely different story, made up by Emperor Constantine and the old bishops. They had excellent imagination. At the Meeting of Bishops in Nicaea in 325 and also at the Meeting of Priests in Constantinople during the sixth century, everything disappeared from the annals that the Fathers of the Church found offensive, mysterious, or questionable. They really have succeeded in keeping people unaware of many interesting Truths until now. The power always takes the greatest part of the glory, as you might know. It is time for a change."

"But how do you know?" I asked. "Where am I? Is this not the Garden of Gethsemane? Are you not the so-called Jesus the Christ or Messiah?"

"Of course I am. For you and your contemporaries, all this happened very long ago. But now you are visiting me in order to hear the Truth from me more vividly. What could be better for you than experiencing situations from mine and Mary Magdalene's life? It will be living evidence, and you can take part in it yourself."

"From the beginning?" I asked eagerly.

"Oh yes, I can tell about my life from the beginning, a somewhat different story from what you have heard. We can sit down here, under one of the old cedars, and I will tell you my story. Your Bible tells it its way; I'll tell it my way! You may ask questions if you want to. You will see images when I touch your forehead. Is that all right?"

I nodded. It was unbelievable and wonderful to hear Jesus Christ talking. The whole gathering of people sat down on the grass and Mary Magdalene sat close to her husband with her head on his shoulder. Little David hid his head in his mother's lap and soon fell asleep. It was just before dusk. Daylight faded and formed a bluish shimmering light that caressed every participant's forehead and obscured their eyes. Jesus' eyes were the only ones that glistened and glowed in the approaching evening. He signed to me to sit near him on his other side, so as to be able to listen to him without any disturbances.

"I was not engendered by the Holy Spirit or an Angel. The Immaculate Conception is something that those Bible-writers at the Bishop Meeting in Nicaea invented. They wrote that, because otherwise I could be considered a bastard or illegitimate. And maybe I was!" Jesus laughed and so did I.

I asked, "Who was your father?"

"I'm not ready to reveal that – yet. I will tell you later." He looked sad, and I think I saw some bitterness in his strange eyes. "People cannot embrace it. As I told you before, Christianity is built on a lie that humanity has taken to their hearts. If we gave them the Truth with all its convolutions, it would seem a lie to them. Two thousand years of indoctrinated knowledge needs time to be changed and digested. For the present I can only tell you that there were good reasons for Joseph to marry my mother, despite the fact that he was so much older than her. They both were Essenes. I always looked on Joseph as my own father in the flesh and my brothers and sisters as my own siblings in the flesh.

"On my twelfth birthday my mother told me the Truth about my birth and why I had such an important mission. Before that I was just a member of a big family. We children quarreled, played, and made jokes, as all children do. I was hungry for knowledge and I snatched up everything I could everywhere. I was curious about life both outside and inside of humans. From birth my inner life was well developed, because I pondered the great questions, that required answers, in my thoughts. But I also talked to somebody, somebody who slowly and patiently answered my questions. Somebody who was invisible, but yet present.

"I have always loved animals. It was unusual to care about animals other than cattle during those days, since the Jews looked upon animals as unclean. I have memories from the age of five or six." (He touched my forehead and I saw clear images of what he was telling me.) "Already at that time I looked upon animals as parts of group souls. There is a group soul for every kind of animal, and when people talked about soulless animals it hurt my heart. Don't ask me who whispered the knowledge in my ears about the group souls. Surely it was my Father in Heaven.

"One day I was walking among the trees that surrounded our house. Suddenly I saw a little bird lying on the ground. I picked it up and held it in my hand. It was cold, stiff, and appeared dead. Its eyes were closed and its heart wasn't beating anymore. I was so sad that I started to cry. I caressed the little bird and wished from the bottom of my childish heart that life would be brought back to it. Suddenly it started to move. I carefully caressed its head and heart and thanked my Father in Heaven. The bird rose cautiously, shook its wings, and flew away, but first it softly caressed my face with its wing. It thanked me.

"After that I often heard it singing nearby and I knew it was saying 'Thank you!' I never feared any animals, and I actually could talk to them and make contact with their group souls. This included all kinds of animals, from the biggest animal to the smallest insect.

"We lived in Galilee. In the year 164 BC Galilee was looked upon as a nation of heathens where only few Jews still lived. In the year 103 BC Aristobulos, the first king of the Jews, forced everyone living in Galilee to adopt the law of Moses and the men be circumcised. It meant that all children, at a certain age, formally had to convert to the Jewish creed and to go to the synagogue in order to be examined before admission. My parents were Aryans and mystics because of their philosophical way of thinking and Jews because of a forced adoption. The old capital of Galilee with its hot springs was called Hamath. They did not talk Hebrew in Galilee. I learned Aramaic and Greek.

"I have been called the Nazarene, and people say that Nazareth was the city of my birth. When I was born, there was no city called Nazareth. Three hundred years after my birth the city Nazareth was proclaimed because the Fathers of the Church had to have a name for my birthplace. Jan, you must understand now that posterity was very much cheated in many ways. The Jews called all foreign nationalities and religions Nazarenes in the same way that you, in modern times, talk about blacks if people have a darker complexion than another. In fact, Nazarene was an abusive word. But the worst problem was that they confused the words Nazarene and Essene. In the Bible it is written that I returned to the city of Nazareth. The more correct formulation would be that I returned to the Nazarenes. Both of my parents were forced to formally remain in the Jewish church, even if they were Essenes.

"When I first heard the Truth about my lineage, I was shocked. I belonged to the house of David – I was a royal offspring! It was because of the after-effects of that shock that I stayed in the temple with the wise old men. When my parents came to pick me up from there, my father was advised to send me to Qumran. Joseph was a skillful carpenter and he had taught me his profession. But as I grew older I felt that it was no profession for me. I knew that I had the gift of healing. Every day

I talked to my Father in Heaven, who now became my only Father. Joseph understood, but he suffered. To my inexpressible joy my cousin John the Baptist went with me to Qumran. We were about the same age. John was six months older than me and we had shared our sorrows and problems from childhood. We were both cosmically conscious. We could talk to each other about everything; we could penetrate each other's deepest thoughts and help one another to understand.

"A laborious period of my life started. The Essenes have wonderful thoughts and knowledge, but they have a strict discipline. John and I could share our experiences only in the few moments when we were allowed a little freedom. I felt a big desire to travel around the world. What we learned about the world made me curious to see other countries; new people and different places. John was a true ascetic. We wanted the same thing but in different ways.

"Everything was well arranged in Qumran. There were vast spaces for walking and, remarkably enough, lots of flowers, in spite of the lack of water. The hard discipline was beneficial for us boys. There are many traditions that still survive in your Christianity that we brought with us from Qumran, my cousin and I. But John did not stay there for long. He had other tasks. I very much liked the old custom of the Holy Communion because it ties people together and creates a unity. We didn't do it exactly as you do it today. We didn't compare the wine with blood or the bread with flesh. For us wine and bread were symbolic in another way: the wine was cosmic energy and the bread was cosmic nutrition. Do you understand?"

I nodded and felt angry about all the symbols our priests are using. They are indeed misinterpreting the whole thing.

"I don't like the Holy Communion," I added. "All this stuff about eating your flesh and drinking your blood seems cannibalistic to me." Jesus laughed. I went on: "I bet you don't know that the Holy Communion derives from a time long before your life on Earth, in fact from the dark days of heathendom."

"What do you mean?" Jesus was upset and he continued. "The Holy Communion is very old and truly Essene. I will make myself clear: The wine represented the divine essence and the bread was the physical, life-preserving food. I learned that in Qumran. So you really mean the Holy Communion is a heathen invention?"

"Yes," I answered, "it really is. During the time of the Celts and the Druids in England and Ireland people sacrificed animals. There's even talk about human sacrifices. The sacrificed animal was always eaten after the ritual. It was the Celts who decided this and the Druids unwillingly accepted it, in order to keep their power. The sacrificed animal was considered to represent the divinity at the meal. While eating it, you and your fellow-believers entered the mystical divine society, and you and the god became one. What do you say about that?"

"Poor people," sighed Mary Magdalene in a tired voice. "Ignorance sows evil seeds. But please go on telling us, dear husband. We don't have the whole night."

"I need not go into details about the years at Qumran," Jesus went on. "It was simply a school. They wanted to keep me there as a teacher when my studies were finished, but I was not interested. I wanted to see the world. I knew that my gifts of healing were rare, and I decided to use them in the best way. It was my Father who worked through me. I had learned so much at Qumran – all the good old knowledge of the Essenes. Now I wanted to convey that knowledge and all the wisdom inside me that longed to come out in a shout of joy that everybody should hear. I wanted to convey the Truth."

9. Jesus Tells the Story of His Journeys

"What is the Truth?" I interrupted.

Mary Magdalene looked at me and smiled. "The Truth is inside you," she said softly. "It dwells inside all people if they only listen."

"What do you mean?" I asked, even if I could guess the answer.

"She means that my Father and I are part of all of you," said Jesus. "We dwell in everyone who seeks us. Because we are a part of you, the answers are always there, inside of you."

"But the answers are different," I protested.

"Not if you listen carefully," Jesus insisted. "There is only one answer to each question. Perhaps you're listening in the wrong way."

"How will I know if I listen the right way?"

"You will know," Mary Magdalene put in with a small laugh. "The whole you will feel it. It is both reason and love for Truth that collaborate."

"Yet the answers are so different," I repeated. "Why?"

"Every man is unique," Jesus said. "Every answer suits the unique man."

"Yes, but then they must suit different perceptions and different religions," I objected. "Otherwise there will still be fighting about the Truth."

"Here we go again." Jesus smiled. "The Truth shall set you free, not force you into a dead-end. It is associated with your intuition, but how many of us listen to that?"

I thought for a while. "What about obsessions," I said at last, "that don't allow anything else in and can be compared to a bloodsucking tick …"

"We're getting away from the question if we are going to discuss deviations," Jesus interrupted. "In every human being there is a part of the Divine. It has only one face, only one answer, only one great, profound feeling. Humans must try to attain this Divinity. This is the answer that disappeared in the technical development, but still is a part of every DNA and still dwells quietly in the deepest hiding-place of your cells. This is exactly what must be freshened up again. You sometimes called me the Fisherman. Then I will teach you where the best fishing-waters are: namely in your own soul."

"Stop! Now you're muddling up DNA and soul …"

"Of course not. Everything is associated when the shell has been removed."

"What do you mean by shell? Death?"

"No, my dear visitor from the Angelic Realm! Your thoughts are like swift birds, driven by the wind. The shell is the outer human being living in society, involving himself with power, money, and politics, etc. That thin shell must be removed. The time has come now."

"Okay. That will cause problems," I sighed. "The Truth has to be awakened in every individual. Everyone has his own Truth and it is utterly hopeless. Look how things are on Earth! How can you help the whole of humanity to find the right way?"

"You are interviewing me about my life now, Jan. There is only one Truth about it."

"Don't you meet many traitors on your way?"

"Of course, but you must learn to separate the wheat from the chaff …"

I interrupted him quickly with a question. "Who are you, really?"

"The one your heart tells you I am. I am a part of your innermost being, a part of what constitutes your soul."

"Science on Earth today tries to explain away the soul." I felt I had to get to the bottom of this. I felt we were getting away from the reason for my visit to Gethsemane and were embarking on an unknown journey in several senses. I could perceive the quiet breathing of Lydia, but she did not talk. Apparently she did not want to be seen; she wanted to observe without being observed.

"No words or theories will help there. The soul is and remains the strongest element in what is you. The soul speaks through your heart. So, listen to your heart, follow its rhythm, and breathe in its energies."

"What happens if you replace your heart, then? Heart transplants are said to be common on Earth nowadays."

"You cannot replace the inner energy, only alter it. If, for instance, you replace the water pump in your house, the same water as before will run through the new pump. You also have the power of thought, that nobody can destroy. It is associated with the cosmic energy of your heart. It is important to get the inner prerequisites, the inner powers, to cooperate. If you can do that, you protect yourself, even if you replace your heart. At the same time, you must allow for new impulses and other energies that have come with your new heart. But, my dear Jan, we were going to study the Truths of your Bible, not the inner life of humans."

"Well, then, tell me about your journeys after you left Qumran," I asked him.

"They were rather extensive." Jesus smiled and patted a shaggy dog, lean and frightened, that approached him. Mary Magdalene searched the numerous folds of her robe and found a piece of bread that she gave to the dog. It sat down at once near us and munched. Something in this simple action moved me deeply. Perhaps it was her beautiful face, radiating love, or perhaps it was her quiet movements when she fed the animal. Perhaps it was the eyes of the grateful dog when he looked at her. I felt she was a woman a man could die for. I was proud to be able to escort her on the long journey. Jesus observed my reaction and said, "No human being and no animal is too insignificant to be embraced by Love. Those wise words I brought with me from Qumran, when I was heading towards India as my first destination.

"Jagannath is situated on the east coast of India. Today it is called Puri. It took me an adventure-packed year to get there, and that is why I stayed there for about a year. I had a teacher who also became my loyal friend. His name was Lamaas, and I persuaded him to go to Palestine later on, in order to join the Essenes there.

"My next destination was the Ganges valley. I lived for a while in Benares. There were schools which – during my days – were famous for their high culture. The Hindus were skillful in curing diseases, and there I learned healing which I practiced often after that. I didn't think people had the right to be ill. I was interested in finding out why sickness and illness existed. Was it a punishment or contagion, or was it genetic? The answer is related to your way of thinking. The power of thought is creative – but you surely know that.

"In Benares, where I continued my journey, I learned to teach and to use parables and narratives. The Hindus, though, forbade me to teach and asked me to stop visiting the lower castes. I really made some enemies there! The way of thinking of the Hindus is difficult to cope with in many ways. To me all people are equal, and I find it utterly wrong to divide them into castes.

"After Benares I went to Persia. It was a thrilling country. I studied in Persepolis and I made many friends there. Magic was one of my main topics, white Magic …"

"When did you meet Mary Magdalene?" I interrupted.

"Don't rush things. I will tell you in time. In Persia I received and laid the foundation of the principles of meditation. I channeled – as you call it – my Father in Heaven and several great Masters. I learned how to divide my soul from my body and visit other worlds.

"Euphrates was my next destination. I went around and visited several towns in Chaldea and in the countries between Euphrates and Tigris. It was difficult to leave the ruins of Babel, where memories of amphibians were imprinted in gray boulders. You must know that Babel was founded by an amphibian, Oannes, who came from the stars and brought great wisdom and ability to the people living there."

"I thought that was a fairy-tale," I answered. "Have you seen any amphibians?"

"Yes, I have. I know they are here, still visiting Earth," Jesus maintained seriously. "I think they will be needed in a distant future, a long time after the one you come from. But that is another story."

Now and then Jesus touched my brow and I saw an image, like a mirage, of what he told me. It is difficult to explain if I saw the images in the air surrounding me or inside me.

Jesus went on, "Then I went to Egypt. My last destination was Heliopolis, where I was to be trained for the higher stages of the Great White Brotherhood. It consists of Ascended Masters who are intended to lead Earth. Unfortunately, people's free will has taken over, and they are not considered Masters any longer. They dwell in another Reality, but also sometimes on Earth. They had one of their earthen temples in Heliopolis. The other one is situated in Tibet. I studied keenly in Heliopolis for many years, but I also wrote a lot. I liked to write and I wrote as much as I could."

"Where are your scriptures?" I eagerly asked. "Is it still possible to find them?"

He shook his head. "Not all of them. Some of them were burned in the big library fire in Alexandria, but some are hidden in a safe place. I readily wrote about symbolic deeds. I went through initiations in Heliopolis that made a huge impact on me and inspired me to write. The Sun Temple, that was also a high-school, was magnificent. It was surrounded by splendid sphinx-avenues and remarkable obelisks. That place was really inspiring.

"You can say that half of my power was a divine, innate gift and the other half was developed by studies, exercises, and experiences. Every human has this Divine power inside, but few care to develop it. Even at that time, I maintained that some magicians can cure illness and wake the dead and that that kind of healing will come in the future. Illness and suffering are abnormal conditions and I taught how the body would be relieved of suffering and how the mind would harmonize with Natural Law. Doesn't that sound almost modern, Jan?"

"Yes, it really does. But your journeys so far do not include your travels with your mother, do they? Some scriptures tell about that."

"I did travel to Alexandria with my mother before going to Qumran. I was twelve, and thirteen the Spring afterwards. We did that journey in order to prepare for my studies there and in Heliopolis and for my meeting with the old teachers. They didn't want to teach naughty, ignorant boys who wanted to study there for worldly reasons, to get a feather in their cap, as you say. And I did another journey that maybe you never heard of. I went with my brother Joseph of Arimathea to Britain to a place that is called Glastonbury."

"Then it is true!" I exclaimed happily. "Why did you go there?"

"Joseph was a tradesman who was trading in metals. There was a lead mine in the Mendip Hills, and when we visited it we were advised to go further on to Glastonbury. Already at that time it was a holy place. We met some interesting people there. At the time there were Celtic Druids in Glastonbury, and those priests had an extensive knowledge of magic and culture from very ancient times. They laid a foundation in me for something that I developed further in subsequent trips."

"Is there a similarity to the Essene and the Druid faiths?" I eagerly asked.

"Oh yes, really!" Jesus smiled, and I almost thought I saw mischief in his eyes. "Because, my dear friend, there is only one Truth, even if it develops in different ways."

"Can you explain what you mean?"

"The Druids are called heathens. It is said that their culture is heathen. But I think there is much Christianity in their faith. The highest Druids, who are also called saronites, are initiated in the inner mysticism. The priests are called vates or ovates. Next come the eubages who are astrologers and skilled fortune-tellers. The augures study medicine, including anatomy."

"Are they that advanced?" I exclaimed.

"Yes, but they are threatened with extinction," Jesus sighed. "There are still some of them left, but they will gradually disappear. Yet I don't think they will totally disappear, even if they stay in the background. Their teaching, their strong soul, is too powerful for that. But let's go back to my later travels."

"Would you like to tell about those initiations in Heliopolis, or are they secret?"

"Not all of them. I lived for a while with good friends near the monastery school in Heliopolis. I was to spend three months of peace, prayer, and meditation there as a preparation for my final examination. I was expecting the Master of the Brotherhood to visit me in a psychic way and I felt full of anticipation. But it didn't happen as I had imagined.

"One night, at midnight, I was awakened by the sound of somebody opening the door to my room. A priest came in, wearing an official oriental dress. He tried to make me change my plans. He warned me not to stay in Egypt, because my mission was seen as a threat against the priesthood of Egypt. There were plans to kill me or to put me into jail. The priest offered me several different ways to escape from Egypt in order for me to return to Palestine. I answered him that I would not sell my soul for the safety of my body. I knew my mission on Earth, and I was going to remain true to my Father in Heaven. The priest looked at me in a queer way and went out as silently as he had come.

"The next day I was called to meet the representatives of the Brotherhood in the monastery. The Hierophant, who was the highest priest, put his hand lovingly on my head and gave me a strip on which was written the word 'Sincerity.' The Brotherhood appreciated that I was never tempted to escape from my mission.

"Some weeks later a stranger visited me. He told me something very interesting. He claimed he had gone through the same training as I had and that he had suffered afflictions and enmity from the priesthood of Egypt, yet he had stayed because he wanted to fulfill his mission. But he became severely shocked when he was allowed to partake in secret meetings and ceremonies. Their rites were sheer devil worship. They had sacrificing parties where they killed innocent children and young women and burned them as a sacrifice to their false gods. He had succeeded in escaping them and he urged me to flee before it was too late. I felt vexed and annoyed and told him he was a traitor and there was no way I would listen to more of that rubbish.

"The next day, again I met the Hierophant and got a new strip on which was written 'Justice.' This was my second initiation. The third one came a month later.

"I was sitting in the Temple, meditating, when a priest came to me. He praised me and told me what a good teacher and healer I was and how important my mission was. He claimed that I ought to leave

Heliopolis and organize a priesthood myself, that would surpass all others and bring me wealth, glory, and unlimited power.

"This was really a challenge. But when I listened to my inner voice it told me clearly that I had to follow the mission given me by my Father in Heaven. I thanked the priest because he had awakened a struggle inside me, but my mission was to serve and believe, not to strive after wealth and power.

"Again the Hierophant called me and gave me another strip with 'Faith' written on it. I had gotten through the first three stages of initiation. The rest are secret, but I passed them and was honored with the title 'Master.' Do you want me to tell you about the last initiation in the Cheops pyramid?"

"Yes, please!" I was delighted. I heard a quiet, cautious snicker from nowhere, and I understood that Lydia too was delighted. But her laugh was heard by somebody else.

"You have company!" Jesus exclaimed with a smile. "Tell your companion to emerge. I presume it is another Angel? Angels are welcome here."

Lydia slowly emerged. Mary Magdalene rose and gave her a hug. "Now please stay visible with us," she asked. "I understand that in some way you protect Jan. You are welcomed to follow us on our trip."

Lydia sighed, relieved. Maybe it wasn't always fun to be invisible and not be allowed to talk, I thought. My companion sat down at my side, in front of Mary Magdalene. These two immediately became friends.

"I hope you know about the Sphinx," Jesus continued. "Between his gorgeous paws there is a secret passage. The paws rest on high ground, and in the middle there is a small yard with an altar. Behind this altar, just below the chest of the Sphinx, there is a hidden door that can only be opened with a secret code. From there you enter a long subterranean passage under the sand and under the Sphinx. It culminates in a big reception room under the area that surrounds the Cheops pyramid.

"It was midnight when they took me to this room. From there a passage led up inside the pyramid and there was a little chamber on every level. The final ceremony took place in such a chamber, in about the middle of the pyramid. I was dressed in a purple cloak, and when I entered the chamber a royal crown was imprinted on my head. I am not very fond of such magnificence, but I had to endure it because it was symbolic. The room was lit with candles and torches. A white dove floated down from the light and landed on my head. That felt wonderful.

"The Hierophant was sitting at a stone table. He rose when bells started to ring. 'This is Jesus Christ!' he proclaimed, and after that I was acknowledged as an incarnation of the Word, or the living Logos. Afterwards we went down to the big room where Holy Communion, as I explained it to you, was celebrated as a symbolic festivity. All the priests from the Temple school were present. It was extraordinarily solemn. I cannot tell you what was discussed there; it is secret. But from that moment I was ready for my holy mission."

"How did you get back to Palestine?" I asked. "How did your mission start?"

"The Angelic reporter is at work." Lydia laughed, and so did Mary Magdalene. Jesus smiled.

"There was a regular boat-traffic between Egypt and Palestine," he said. "But my mission really started with the Baptism."

10. Jesus Discovers Mary Magdalene

"John the Baptist, my beloved cousin, had come to Palestine for a certain task. He was a wandering soul; he preached and baptized wherever he went. He had changed from the neat student in Qumran to a driving spirit, dressed in a coarse cloak made of camel-hair. Camel-hair is the symbol for humility. He had a purpose in coming here, a purpose which he intended to realize in the Jordan valley.

"There was a lake, called the Lake of Loneliness, where the Essenes used to have their ceremonies and also founded their communities. John prepared people for the coming of the Messiah. People came and they pitched their camps around the lake. They were waiting for the Savior to show up. The shores around the lake were rough and rather inhospitable after volcanic eruptions, but that did not matter when you were waiting for the Savior. John demanded that everyone who felt worthy of rebirth and redemption would get baptized in the water of the lake. His thunderous voice was heard in the still air and reached all trembling, expectant hearts.

"I had not the slightest idea what he was preparing. I only wanted one thing, and that was to be reunited with my dear relative and childhood friend. I was dressed in a modest gray cloak with a hood, which I swept around my body, so as not to be recognized when I sneaked through the crowd on the shore. John was standing in the water near the shore, preaching. But when he saw me he acted in a very odd way. Normally we would have hugged each other, kissing each other on both cheeks. John greeted me as Christ, not as his friend and cousin Jesus. He commanded me to submit myself to baptizing, so I waded out to him. At that moment the rays of the Sun had reached to the very spot where we stood, and they encircled us with their radiant light. John spoke the holy sacrament of the Baptism.

"Thereafter I happened to turn around. It was like an invisible power that forced me to do it; I felt that someone was there. My eyes met a slender, beautiful young girl with long, reddish hair. She was standing on the shore near to us and she held a big white dove. Silently and softly she threw the dove towards me. The dove flew to me and landed on my shoulder while I was standing, keenly watching the young girl. The Sun was shining on her too; she had a halo of shimmering sunbeams around her hair and she smiled and looked at me. I bet you can guess who she was?"

I nodded and looked at Mary Magdalene. She laughed and said, "I had really trained that dove! I was afraid it was going to land on the wrong shoulder, but it didn't. The power of thought is wondrous and it is very effective on animals."

"For me, the Baptism was a double experience," said Jesus. "I felt for the first time in my life the burning flames of human love and the Holy Ghost entering my soul. I believe none of that is mentioned in your Bible."

Lydia and I laughed heartily, and it felt good to be spared the solemnity and rigor that the Bible attributed to Jesus. It was comforting to see that humanness had a prominent role also during the first part of our current era.

"How were your forty days in the desert, which were said to occur after the Baptism?" I asked.

"Don't take it literally," Jesus answered. "I was not in the desert for forty days; it's only a symbolic phrase. The Brotherhood of the Essenes often use the number forty. It must have slipped into the Bible. I went to a calm place where I was alone, meditating for a couple of weeks. I needed that after my hard studies and long journeys. I had to prepare for my great mission: to heal and to preach like my cousin John. But I couldn't forget the woman with the dove, though. I had seen people I knew standing next to her, so I could ask them for her name. I wanted to know where she got the idea of the dove, so I visited her," Jesus said, and made a gesture to Mary to continue.

"I knew about Jesus long before he knew about me," she said, smiling. "I knew when he returned from Egypt. I also knew Martha and Mary in Bethany. They never stopped talking about Jesus. I knew his mother, too, and she got letters from her son now and then, even if the postal service was slow. From Alexandria it was more regular; the letters came by boat. Mary from Bethany read his letters to me and to anybody who wanted to listen, and those letters reached out to me. I knew I had to meet him. I loved him long before I had seen him. I trained the dove for fun, but I hoped to be able to use it when Jesus was baptized. There was a rumor that John the Baptist was going to baptize his cousin on that very day, so I hurried off with my dove to the Lake of Loneliness. My husband told you the rest."

"Soon after that I asked her to marry me," continued Jesus, and took his wife's hand. "We had a secret wedding with only our closest relatives present. There were no great celebrations as is customary; we wanted it like that.

"Have you read my Sermon on the Mount? In fact, a great part of it is true, even if the gospels interpret it differently. In the Sermon on the Mount I taught four important principles: humility, caring for others, the inner goodness of the heart, and living righteously. These principles my wife and I always have tried to obey."

"Please tell me about all your miracles," I said. "Did they happen like it says in the Bible?"

"Not very much happened like it says in the Bible," Jesus answered seriously. "If you mean my supernatural so-called miracles, I don't know what to answer. Certain healings occurred outside the boundaries of the Laws of Nature, but to me all laws are divine and I have many years of extensive education and training in healing. I simply used my God consciousness. If you regard illness and suffering as something abnormal in the human body, you can also learn how to remove it, provided that you use the Cosmic Laws."

"How did you do that trick with the bread and the fishes?" I asked irreverently. "Can you conjure up food, just like that?"

Jesus smiled again. "No," he answered. "All that is invention and exaggeration. You can't imagine how many inventions about me are written in your Bible. I know how to 'precipitate' – that means how to generate something seemingly out of thin air. I only do it when it is urgently needed. What is described in your Bible, however, is an act of sorcery that fills me with disgust. Why should I conjure up all that food? If I had really done that, it would have indicated that I used the principles of self-assertion and boasting; that is not at all nice and would not have followed my golden rules.

"'The bread and the fishes' only had a symbolic meaning, but something happened that made it more realistic. A little child came to me with his package of food, which consisted of fish and bread. 'Here you are,' he said. 'Eat my food if you are hungry.' It was at that moment I got the idea. I asked everyone who had brought food with them to share with those who hadn't. In this way all of them were fed, because of the generosity of this little lad."

I was astonished. "Are there more things in the Bible that you haven't done?" I stammered.

Jesus began to laugh. "You bet there are! Ask me what I really did, instead of what is true in the Bible."

"What about the twelve disciples? Did they exist?" I was frightened and startled.

"Yes, but I had many more disciples, both men and women. Mary Magdalene was one of them, and at the same time she was a teacher. She was there all the time. Nobody had reason to be jealous, because all men obeying Jewish law had to marry when they reached a certain age. Most of my disciples were married – Peter, Mark, Matthew, Simon, and John the Beloved. Thomas married young and became a young widower. He was a true disciple until the Crucifixion, but after that he followed my namesake Jesus, or Issa."

"Do you mean that your marriage is not mentioned in the Bible, although it meant punishment not to be married?" I interrupted. "Were these bishops in Nicaea misogynists, all of them?"

"Probably," was the dry answer. "You are cheated; the whole of Christianity is taken in, and it is not my fault. These bishops were not the slightest bit better than Mohammed and his like when it comes to disparaging women. In a way, I think people cheat themselves by believing what they want to believe. I didn't preach for the benefit of Christianity, churches, and priests. I preached what I found to be in accordance with my heart and what I found good in all the teachings and wisdom I had learned since I was a little boy. I didn't intend it to be preached in a church. The Church and Christianity is not me – it's the invention of the priests."

"And what about the Old Testament?"

"I'm not interested in discussing it. There are some true historical events in it, but the God mentioned there is not my God. My Father in Heaven is loving and merciful."

"Shall we go on with your miracles? Was it really okay to awaken Lazarus from the dead?"

"You must understand that people at that time were very superstitious. If a person was lying quite motionless and seemed not to breathe, he was dead. Lazarus was not dead. What is written about his putrefaction is not true, it is only the spice of an untrue story. Lazarus was in a coma. They often made the mistake of confusing coma with death at that time. Many people were buried alive if a doctor or a healer of some kind was not available. I recognized Lazarus' illness and I could awaken him from the coma with healing. The Bible writers were using this because they knew that people's superstitions would bid it up to something supernatural."

"Did Mary Magdalene follow you on your wanderings? Did she witness you walking on the water? How did you do that?"

"Yes, Magdalene accompanied me on most wanderings, but not all. And I must admit that I walked a few steps across the surface of the water. Skilled magicians in India know how to do that and I learned some magic from them. I can tell you that it is simply a thought-phenomenon. Whoever wants to walk on water and is able to concentrate his thoughts can do it. Another miracle, isn't it?"

I nodded, but I wanted to know more. "The Gospel according to Thomas has been found. On one page it says that Peter, the male chauvinist, wanted to remove Mary Magdalene from the disciples. Your answer, according to Thomas, was that you were going to make a man of her. What do you mean by that?"

"I mean that your translations are absolutely wrong! Why would I turn my beloved wife into a man? I remember that my answer to Thomas was something like this: 'If women were men, no women would exist. They are a part of the wholeness, and their tasks are not only to bear children and manage the household, but also to complete the male, who couldn't exist without the female. A world with only men would be a dead world.' I asked the disciples to respect their women and also appreciate their way of thinking. To be the servant of God doesn't include belittling women. That is a silly way of thinking.

"My wife is not only beautiful and intelligent, but also a very skillful healer. She has worked at my side all the time, but the people don't count her, because she is a woman. She doesn't work with magic, but she heals a lot of people. Without her I would never have succeeded in my difficult mission, and I think she came down to Earth in order to be my wife."

"Would you like us to proceed directly to your worries regarding the coming days, or do you want to say something else before that?"

"We don't have much time. I think I have told you the necessary things about my life so far. Therefore we can skip what's written in the Bible about the time before they arrested me. Mary Magdalene and I worked all the time from early morning to sunset. She wants to stay here now and support me in the coming difficulties, but I can't allow it. Take good care of her, Jan, and make sure our child is born under good circumstances."

Angels don't wear watches, but I understood it was time now to leave Gethsemane and walk the long way to the harbor. Angels don't have any luggage either, but Mary Magdalene did. Two young men, probably disciples, came with us and carried the luggage. Mules were waiting outside the herb garden. Lydia took Mary's arm so she would not stumble in the increasing darkness.

11. Jesus and the Merchants in the Temple

"There is something I really would like to see while I'm now looking for the Truth," I said when I met Kualli again. "I wonder if the Bible gives a true picture of Jesus when he was furious with the merchants in the Temple in Jerusalem. I thought Jesus was all humility and mildness."

"It happened that his angry temper could prevail when he witnessed injustices," Kualli laughed. "Well, I can send you there, as an odd interlude."

Lydia immediately took my hand and we slipped into the usual fog. Suddenly we were in the heart of Jerusalem, at the square outside the big Temple. I was dressed in my usual monk's habit, but Lydia was wearing a gaudy colored dress, made of patches in various colors in a beautiful pattern. Where did she find her clothes? She must have read my thoughts, because she laughed. We were both materialized now.

"I create my clothes with the help of my thoughts," she explained and put a gray-green shawl over her shoulders that she had carried under her arm. "You'd better merge with the crowd here. Look around, Janne!"

The market-place was immense, and people were pushing and jostling each other. You have to get used to that in this country, I thought. The odor of smoke, sweat, and aromatic oils was almost overpowering. Between the pillars was the entrance to the Temple, lined with many different merchants. There were dove-sellers, money-changers, and a bit further inside the yard were the sacrificial animals. Lydia pinched my arm hard, and I turned around angrily. There was Jesus, followed by a lot of disciples. He made his way through the crowd, and people made way for him. His face expressed a violent rage and his arms were outstretched. He held rope and scourge in his hands.

Jesus went straight to the dove-sellers and broke the birdcages into pieces. The terrified doves flew away, scattered in all directions. After that he threw over the tables of the money-changers, banging things wherever he could. Floods of coins fell to the ground, and the horror-struck merchants ran away in different directions. The beggar-children grabbed as many coins as they could find. It all happened very swiftly.

Jesus cried, "The doves pollute my Father's house. You have made the house of prayer into a robbers' den!" He was striking out and gesticulating wildly like a warrior. This was his war. His war against Mammon and against the disrespect for the Divine. But I'll never forget the expression on his face at that moment. A beautiful face distorted by rage is no longer beautiful, yet there was a brilliant radiance because of the just and pure intention.

"The Pharisees and the scribes are sitting on Moses' chair!" he cried, standing in front of the Temple. The priests hastened forth to hear what the troublesome disturber of the peace had to say, before they started to stone him. It was not the first time they'd stoned him, but he always got away without a single scratch.

"Woe betide you, scribes and Pharisees!" he continued. "You are hypocrites who devour widows' houses while you pretend to preach in the Temple. You are dressed in beautiful clothes, but your hearts are full of voluptuousness, hypocrisy, and detestable misdeeds. Woe betide you, scribes, you hypocrites who pay your tithes of mint, dill, and caraway, but exclude the most important things in the law: namely, Love, mercy, and faith. You strain at a gnat and swallow a camel! Ye offspring of vipers, how can you flee from the judgment of hell?"

After that he looked around and added, in a calmer voice, "Jerusalem, Jerusalem, you cruel city which kills prophets and stones holy men walking on your streets. Listen up! Those who believe in me also believe in God, who sent me to carry out His will. You who see me now also see my Father: God. Walk in the Light while it stays with you, so that everybody understands that you are the children of Light. Darkness will come, and then you must be ready to find the way. I have not come to judge the world, but to save it ..."

Stones started to hail against him while he was talking, but then, suddenly, he had disappeared. We looked for him everywhere, but we couldn't find him. Did he hide among his disciples, or had he used magic? I guessed the latter.

"Jesus learned a lot in Tibet," Lydia told me. We made our way to a small dungeon nearby. "Do you know, Jan, that most of the material in his famous Sermon on the Mount derives from Buddhist ethics?"

I shook my head, really surprised. "Has he stolen material from the Buddhists?" I asked disrespectfully.

"Yes!" Lydia nodded her head, and her curls fluttered around her brow, making her look like a little girl. "At the Buddhists' Jesus became a 'bodhisattva,' that is to say, a candidate for the Buddha-ship."

"How do you know?" I quickly asked.

"Dear Jan, I am a religious researcher," she said, smiling. "I know a lot about religion and I find that part very interesting. In what we call Christianity there is a lot of material from the Buddhists. You didn't know that, did you? I don't know if what we call 'the common people' will accept it, but it's the Truth."

"Jesus talked about purgatory and hell," I pondered. "Is that also inherited from Buddhism?"

She nodded again. "Yes, and even more than that. It is a very old, original teaching that has existed from the beginning of life. Jesus brings us no news; he paraphrases the news!"

"What do you mean?" I felt angry. I liked Jesus, and this was more than I could endure. "Do you mean he's bluffing?"

Lydia caressed my cheek. "Of course not. I'm just trying to explain to you that nothing is new under the Sun. The purgatory tradition shows a faith that has at one time been worldwide and that is probably older than the oldest written testimonies from Babylon and Egypt. The same goes for the teaching of reincarnation."

"Is transmigration from Buddha?"

"You mean that a human being can be born as an animal in his next life? Oh no, that absolutely doesn't come from Buddhism or from original Christianity … or whatever the faith was called long before our

Christianity. The flow of human life is always developing. That is one of the most important theses of Buddha. In Egypt they believed that after death you were immobile for 3000 years, but we won't discuss that now. I am eloquent when it comes to my favorite subject: religious research. You must stop me or I will start talking about the collected works of Plato and what the Greek heroes did after death when they chose which bodies they wanted to enter. They could choose man or animal!"

"Goodness gracious, stop it!" I laughed. "This is about Jesus. Don't you think he made a fool of himself here at the Temple?"

"The scene you saw recently happened a few days before he was arrested in Gethsemane," answered Lydia. "His rage was probably very mixed, because he knew he would be imprisoned soon and probably crucified. He showered abuse on the Jews because they were so mean to him. I think he behaved in a very human way."

"Good!" I sighed. "Are we going home now?" I didn't know why, but deep in my heart, grief unfolded its black veil. We had decided to be present at the Crucifixion.

12. The Last Supper and the Role of the Grail

The Last Supper, popular in churches and painted by many great artists, is contested and disputed, and you can question if it really was the last supper Jesus had with his disciples. I was pondering over this question while I was wondering which peep-hole we were going through next time.

"You are absolutely right, Jan," twittered Lydia's happy voice. "We must have a look at the Last Supper. I wonder about the Grail in this context."

"The Grail is still a family heirloom," I muttered. "I'm sure they used it during that very occasion. I wonder if all of them drank from it and if Joseph of Arimathea put the blood of Jesus in it when he was hanging lifeless at the cross during the Crucifixion."

"Of course he didn't!" cried Lydia. "In that case Jesus could have died. The bishops in Nicaea made that up. I will show you!"

Now she was in a hurry. She pushed me through the spheres. That meant that we both had our eyes closed and knew nothing until we got there.

Our Angelic feet had ended up in something resembling a common bar. It was a dark room, with a long table laid at one end. There were several guests sitting at smaller tables.

"This is an Essene tavern," Lydia whispered, and beckoned to me to sit down at a table near an open fire and also near the long table. We were evidently allowed to be visible during this peep-hole trip. I felt the hard, cool earthen floor under my feet, and the table top was very well used. I stared at the long table. I was thinking of da Vinci's painting and other paintings of the Last Supper. What I saw here didn't resemble them, and there were a lot of people, many more than twelve, sitting around the table. I counted twenty-three, but they were constantly moving and it was almost impossible to count them.

Jesus sat in the middle, and on his right side sat pretty Mary Magdalene. This meal must have taken place just before I met them in the Garden of Gethsemane. I also saw Mary from Bethany and her sister and brother with their backs to us. I could name most of the disciples, but it was really difficult to distinguish Judas Iscariot from the other Judas, son of James. They were very similar, both dark, with beards and brown eyes, and they sat near to each other and had a very lively conversation.

"Can you see the Grail?" whispered Lydia. I nodded. Jesus and Mary Magdalene had just drunk out of it. It seemed as if they shared the Grail. The others had small mugs in front of them. It wasn't that strange; it would have taken too long for the Grail to be passed around, I thought. It was rather dark in the room and difficult to make out the extraordinary beauty of the Grail. Suddenly I saw Peter – the big man with light brown hair and cold eyes – snatch the Grail from Mary's hand and drink from it. Jesus observed this and didn't look very happy. He reached for the Grail and knocked on the table with his fist. The murmur ceased and he asked for more wine. A servant – perhaps another disciple – at once came running with a large stone bottle. Obviously, Peter had taken a big sip.

"This is our last meal together," said Jesus, looking around. The young man on his left, John the Beloved, started to sob and leaned against his shoulder. Mary Magdalene took John's hand behind her husband's back and it was suddenly very quiet.

The dark room, lit only by the fire and a few oil-lamps, for a moment seemed to me like Hades, the black entrance to the kingdom of Death. The lights faded and people clung together for consolation. Evil was not permitted to enter, but it lurked somewhere outside and waited for a chance to penetrate the messenger of Light, the true herald of Light. The reflection of the fire played on the wooden pillars that held the roof. Between the roof-beams unseen wings fluttered. Maybe it was bats or just small birds who were looking for shelter there. The silence played tag with the darkness and the uncertainty.

"I will always be there with each one of you who preaches the gospel of Love," Jesus went on and lifted the Grail. "Let this chalice pass around among all those who understand that my flesh is inferior to my spirit and that my spirit, as all of yours, has eternal life."

The Grail was passed around the table. It was refilled and continued around the whole hall. (We, Lydia and I, also drank from it now that we were materialized.) On the main table were bread and dried mutton, ewe's-milk cheese, honey-cakes, and vegetables.

Jesus took a large loaf of bread, broke off a piece of it, and said, "Eat a piece of this holy bread, which is given to you by the infinite grace of God. He, not you, is the one to see that bread is on your table." He gave it to John, who broke off a piece and passed it on further. Many loaves of bread were needed, but Jesus blessed them all before they were eaten.

I had not imagined the Last Supper like this. In our churches they mention "my body" and so on, and I always felt a little cannibalistic when the priest gave the communion in the "Christian" way. Because of that, I refused it when I was quite young. The Truth was not what is written in the Bible. It actually felt good. (When the bread danced away to the small tables, Lydia and I took a fairly big piece in order to make sure that it was bread and not body.)

The atmosphere had become somewhat gloomy. We saw that the disciples were talking eagerly to Jesus and that he held his arms around his wife on one side and John on the other. Everybody wanted to be comforted. Nobody mentioned the word betrayal, crucifixion, or other punishment. Jesus was the consoler; nobody else took that role. He comforted, infused courage, and he even joked with a couple of desperate disciples.

Mary from Bethany held her head hidden between her arms; her sister Martha had put her arm around her. Only one of the disciples ran away. It could be interpreted as an act of despair. I noticed that it was one of the Judases, but I could not make out which one from where I was sitting.

Some of the disciples drank more wine than they ought to, and that didn't improve the atmosphere. The Grail stood between Jesus and his wife. Suddenly he gave it to her. He turned it over to show it was empty. I heard his words to Mary Magdalene when she, rather frightened, put it into her richly folded dress.

"Make sure that it is taken to the place we have been talking about," he said and kissed her on her cheek. She nodded, in tears, and placed his hand on her heart. I didn't know then that she was pregnant.

The Last Supper turned out to be very different than we had expected. At the same time, I was pleased with that. You can find the tense atmosphere we experienced in every painting of this sad meal. Perhaps it was meant to be happy. Jesus was on his way to a new life. Everyone thought he would die – only his closest friends knew better – or hoped.

We returned to the Angelic Realm with very mixed feelings. To be cheated is never nice, even if the result is positive. And cheated we have been – for two thousand years.

13. The Crucifixion

Like a piece of linen, I was mangled between people struggling up a hill. At the top were two crosses with two nailed human bodies. There was enough space for another in the middle. I understood that this journey had taken me to Golgotha, and I did not feel very happy contemplating the coming event. I heard whispers at first, then they were raised into a crescendo of voices, desperate and triumphant, accusing and grieving. I was swept aside with the crowd around me. They were making way for something … somebody. I was glad to have my monk's habit. People made room for me and I came nearer the sad and dreary procession that came wandering from the city. At the head of it Jesus walked. He was carrying his cross. It was heavy and awkward, and sweat ran down his forehead. He was beaten and bloody, and the happy young man from the other night was not there anymore. Instead, his beautiful eyes reflected grief and melancholy.

I couldn't go on watching this any longer. I hurried to Jesus, seized the back part of the cross, and lifted it. Then a man came and helped me. He said his name was Simon of Cyrene and that he felt great compassion and reverence for the man who was called Messiah. We carried the cross together and the burden of Jesus was relieved.

I heard a well-known voice, "It's kind of you to you help him, but it's not mentioned in the history of the Bible!" The giggle that followed undoubtedly came from my friend Lydia.

At that moment we had reached the place for the Crucifixion. But first the cross must be raised. Meanwhile they put Jesus on a short stake in front of the cross. Simon and I supported him, but a guard sent us away. I will spare the reader the details after that, but Jesus was already falling into a coma. He awoke only once after the cross was raised and said the famous words: "Eli, eli, lama sabachtani!" These words have been translated as "Father, Father, why have you forsaken me?" but this is absolutely wrong. In the secret language of the Egyptian pharaohs it means "Father, Father, you make me free!" I doubt that Jesus, who knew several languages and white magic, could have accused his beloved Father of abandoning him. It doesn't tally with the Jesus I knew.

I was here to experience Truth with my own eyes, and I hoped to be allowed to stay longer on this trip, even if I felt very sorry for Jesus' sufferings on the cross. His mother Mary and Mary from Bethany, sister of Martha and Lazarus, knelt before the cross. They cried. I was wondering if they knew he would survive or if they expected his death. I don't know how long I stood there. Simon of Cyrene stood at my side and I felt Lydia's invisible hand in mine. When I opened my eyes they were taking Jesus down from the cross. He showed no life-signs. Not many of us had stayed; most people had already left. I saw no trace of the disciples. Only the two Marys and a young man, presumably John the Beloved, were kneeling at the cross. They were shooed away, under loud protests.

I supposed that Mary from Bethany was the third woman in Jesus' life. She was mourning her Master, but also the man to whom she gave her physical unrequited love. Time and time again, I realized that all these human traits and energies are missing in the Bible. I was very happy that these biblical characters were alive in a way that has never disappeared: love, warmth, joy, and honesty, but also grief and desperation. This last was exactly what I saw in the pretty face of Mary of Bethany. She looked desperate and was crying all the time. She surely did not suspect that Jesus was still alive. Nor did I, before I saw it with my own eyes.

A tall man, impressive-looking and yet closely resembling his brother, approached the guards that were playing dice, about the few items of clothing Jesus had left. I realized that he was a person in authority, and later I found out it was Joseph of Arimathea. Joseph was with four young men, dressed in white clothes. They carried a stretcher on which they placed Jesus, and I hurried after them with Simon.

"Joseph of Arimathea has gotten permission to bury Jesus in his sepulchral chamber," whispered Lydia. "We will go with him to the grave."

Simon did not come with me to the grave chamber. I don't think he dared. The chamber was well lit by torches. There was a comfortable bed where the body of Jesus was placed. Then they started a healing work whose counterpart I'd never seen before. Two Essene doctors anointed his body with delicious scented oils. Another man in the typical white Essene clothes held the Master's head and forced some liquid between his lips. I did not believe my eyes when Jesus opened his eyes and groaned. In that moment I knew that the story of his survival was the Truth. On that point "wise men" have disagreed down the centuries.

"Who are you, stranger?" asked Joseph of Arimathea, suddenly facing me.

"I come from the Angelic Realm," I answered. "I am here to witness the Truth."

"You've done that all right." Joseph smiled. "Now you have to leave, because we have things to do that are neither for human nor Angelic eyes."

I left the grave chamber. Simon was waiting outside. I decided not to tell him what I had witnessed. Even if Simon seemed to be a nice fellow, things were happening in the crypt that could be fatal for Jesus if they came out.

"They're embalming him," I lied, and Simon seemed quite content with that answer. We said goodbye and he returned to Cyrene. I never saw him again. I stumbled on the rough ground on my way home. I felt that I was reaching the border of dimensions …

Kualli's eyes looked intensively into mine when I woke up in the Angelic dimension.

"You know," was all he said, and I nodded. "You will visit him in Egypt later on," he continued, "but we have other things to do first."

"I don't understand," I protested. "How can I go with Mary Magdalene on that boat and at the same time be at Golgotha and witness the Crucifixion? It happened about the same time, didn't it?"

"For us time doesn't exist, and you know that," a patient Kualli told me. "We take you to different occurrences in history. Usually it's possible to watch history beyond time in a kind of kaleidoscope, but we have given you the ability to, for short time intervals, take part in historical events. Is that difficult to understand?"

"Oh yes," I sighed. "Terribly difficult. But I think it is absolutely thrilling to participate in all this. Where are we going now?"

"As long as the disciples of Jesus were swarming around him, there isn't much to tell. But their story belongs to the life of Jesus, and not many of them knew about his survival. We will see what happened to some of them. And we will visit Paul. Are you not curious about him?"

"I'm born curious," I laughed. "Now I have some exciting moments to look forward to. Shall we go on directly from the Crucifixion at Golgotha?"

"That's exactly what we are going to do!" agreed Kualli. "There will be different stages, yet they have a connection."

I leaned back and closed my eyes. The last thing I felt was Lydia's hand in mine. After that I was again standing in the Garden of Gethsemane and looking around.

14. The Meeting with the Disciples

All of them were there, many more than twelve men. I saw no women. I went to the nearest pupil, an elderly man with a long beard. I greeted him with the words "Peace be with you," which I knew was a typical Jesus-greeting. The man answered with the same words, but he also asked who I was.

"I am Jan from the Angelic Realms," I answered. "I have met your Savior, and he wants me to join you. I know that you meet here in order to confer about what to do next."

"You seem to know a lot," the man said, smiling. "I am Andrew, the brother of Simon Peter, he who is called 'The Rock.' We are going to give one another various tasks. Now it's up to us to pass on the mission of our Savior. Each of us will soon be wandering in different directions in order to tell the Truth."

"Aren't you missing someone?" I asked. "Judas Thaddeus, Jacob's son, left you, didn't he?"

"Yes," Andrew sighed. "He pointed out Jesus to the soldiers and got money for that information. We don't want him with us any longer."

So, that was another Truth, I thought. But the people that were standing in various places in the garden constituted a number that exceeded the usual biblical twelve.

"I am going to talk to some of you, but one at a time," I said. "Can I start with you? What are you going to do next? I mean, when you leave this place."

"I will first go back to my family in Bethsaida and say farewell to them," he answered. "And after that I will go to Greece and preach what Jesus told us."

"Since I come from the future, I know it will be dangerous for you in Greece. You will be crucified on an X-formed cross which will be called after you, the cross of St. Andrew."

"That doesn't bother me now." Andrew answered seriously. "Are you going with me?" I shook my head. "What a pity," Andrew continued. "I could do with the company of an Angel!" He gave me a friendly smile, took my hands, and held them to his brow while he said the words "Peace be with you." Then he swiftly left me. Again, I looked around.

A bit further on, a man was sitting on the grass with his head in his hands. He looked as if he was crying. I went to him.

"That's Thomas," Lydia whispered. "He really needs to be comforted."

I touched his shoulder and he jumped with fright and looked at me. I greeted him as an Essene and he answered with the same words. I told him who I was and sat down at his side. His eyes were red and swollen.

"I feel as if I am alone in the whole world," he muttered. "I can't imagine life without Jesus. I feel drained of wisdom. I am completely empty."

"I understand that you have had a hard time," I comforted him, "but I'm sure your Master would be exceedingly sorry if he could see you now. He believed in all his disciples. You must not deceive him, Thomas. Judas did, and one's enough. You have so much to give, and you must go on with that."

"Thank you," he said, obviously moved. "I feel better now. I think I will visit an old man I know called Simon Zebedee. He is wise and he can surely give me advice about what to do next." He bent forward, kissed me on both cheeks, and then stood up. I saw him walk towards the entrance of the garden. I smiled inside, because I knew his next step. As already mentioned, he would be the one who followed the younger Jesus (Issa) to Kashmir.

A man hurried towards me. He had a beard, and he resembled Andrew. His whole person radiated authority. He said the usual greeting, not without a certain amount of suspiciousness, and I answered him in the same way. Then he asked, "Is it a joke, or are you really an Angel, like my brother Andrew states? He has left us now, and I don't know when I will see him again. I'm Simon Peter."

"And I'm the Angel Jan." I smiled and took his outstretched hands.

"I have come on a visit from the Angelic Realm in order to find the Truth. There are lots of writings about the course of events in the Bible, and only a third of it is true. I can only unveil my identity to certain people, because some would find me crazy and take me for a fraud."

"For certain," nodded Simon Peter. "If you have come down from the Angelic Realm you must have met our Master recently, haven't you?"

I understood he wouldn't believe me if I said no, and perhaps he would take me for a fraud anyway. He was a man who wanted proof. I whispered to Lydia for advice. Her answer was to be visible. She surrounded herself with a white light. Peter withdrew from her.

"I assure you that Jan is an Angel," she said in her clear, ringing voice. "Just as I am."

Peter looked at both of us and I fathomed he was scared. "So, there are women in heaven too?" he finally asked, sullenly. "If Mary Magdalene was here she could certainly explain this."

"Certainly not." Lydia smiled. "I am only showing myself to you because I want redress for Jan. He is really not a fraud. And I believe you are not Mary Magdalene's best friend either?"

Lydia was a bit insolent, I thought contentedly. "If at last you believe us, can you tell us where you are going next?" I asked loudly.

"I am going to preach the teachings of the Master," he sulkily replied. "Perhaps I will go to Rome. Those heathens need Christian words – and not from a woman. Goodbye, Angels!"

With those ironical words and an unfriendly look at Lydia, he abruptly turned on his heels and hurried off to some other men in the herb garden. I looked sadly after him. After many years, his destiny was also going to be sad. The men assembled around him, he was a real leader, and I thought that he would be the one to take over the leadership after Jesus. I had never believed that there were only twelve disciples, and now there was a much bigger number of them here. Twelve was a magic number that the bishops used at the meeting in Nicaea. I wanted to say that to Lydia, but she had disappeared.

A young man came towards me. He had long, curly, hair and a nice face without a beard. His eyes were dreamy and his smile was very friendly. "They say that you are an Angel and a messenger from the Master," he said, and eagerly took both my hands. "My name is John, I was the Master's youngest disciple. Do you have a message for me?"

"You are the disciple who will survive all the others." I smiled at him. "Your life will be long and active. You will write a lot and preach yet more."

"Do you know if Jesus will survive?" John asked, looking deep into my eyes. "There is a rumor that his life has been saved and that he has been brought to a safe place. Why has nobody told me that before? I want to be where my Master is."

"You always will be," I assured him, and gave him a hug. "He is the one who will tell you about your journeys and your mission. You will soon meet him again, And yes, he will survive, but please don't tell the others. Let everyone create their own opinion when you meet. Don't forget that you are endangering Jesus if you tell the secret."

John pressed my hands and answered my hug with one more hug in return and disappeared among the trees with happy eyes. It felt good.

I went up to a man who was observing John when he was leaving me. He was older and had a gray beard. He was about to follow John when I stopped him.

"Are you James, John's brother?" I asked. He nodded. "Then please leave John in peace for a moment. He is feeling very well right now and probably he is walking home, where he will put up with the good news I told him."

"Who are you?" James' face expressed a suspicion I often had to cope with among these guys.

"I am a friend of your Master. I live in the Angelic Realm and I have come down to Earth to look for the Truth."

"What Truth? That our beloved Savior died on the cross?" His voice was bitter and judgmental. "How can you be a friend of the Son of God?"

"Isn't every human being a son or a daughter of God?" I asked softly. "Don't grieve for your Master; you will soon meet him again. Where are you going now?"

"I am going to stay in Jerusalem," the disciple answered sullenly. "My mission is there. I intend to continue where my Savior finished."

"Perhaps he hasn't finished," I said cryptically and stared at James. "He has always talked of eternal life, and yet you think he died on the cross. Can someone really die if he has eternal life?"

"I don't want to listen to your blasphemy," snubbed James and turned around. He didn't look at me; he hurried in the same direction that his brother had taken earlier. I wondered if John the Beloved could keep his secret. I also knew that James would be killed in a cruel way by king Herod Agrippa.

Now another one of the disciples interested me. I was going to try to find Luke, the doctor. I wandered around for a while in the garden and I saw a group of men sitting on the grass. They seemed to be having a lively discussion. I asked if one of them was the disciple Luke. I was lucky. A young man stood up. I pronounced the usual Essene greeting and he answered me with the same words.

"I know your Master Jesus," I said, and noticed how he stiffened. "I know you are a physician."

"I am a healer," Luke answered. "I am an Essene physician. I don't belong to the disciples; I work with herbs, roots, leaves, and such things. What do you want?"

"I am an Angel from the Angelic Realm," I told him. "I bring you a message from your Master that he is pleased to see his friends and disciples very soon."

"Oh really; will he appear on a cloud?" was the sarcastic answer.

"No, you will meet him. He will give each of you suitable tasks."

"Then, why did you come here, Angel?" asked Luke, frowning.

"Because I am looking for the Truth," I answered. "You disciples and friends are very different people. Different, but with one single goal, one single mission. That's why I wonder: Where are the women?"

"The Master sent Mary Magdalene away," he sighed. "She was the most suitable one of us to carry on with his mission. But not all of us like having women among us men. After the Crucifixion it is dangerous to be a follower of the Master. Most of us will probably find another place or another country for our mission. Jesus gave us accurate and elaborate instructions where to go if he doesn't come back. What do you think, Angel? Perhaps you know if he is still alive or not?"

"He will come back," was my prompt answer. "If he is alive or not, if he is a spirit or not, you must find out for yourself. You, Luke, will write a gospel in a couple of years. But I must tell you, if Jesus is alive, he cannot go on as before. The Romans will pursue him, they will kill him at once if they find him alive. I really think you should stop speculating whether his body is still living or not. The important things are his spirit and his teachings. These are the things with eternal life."

"Good boy, Jan!" Lydia whispered in my ear. "You're doing well!"

Luke looked me deep in the eyes. His look was intensive and penetrating. Then he took both my hands and clasped me tenderly.

"Thank you for those words," he said. "I will keep them in my heart and write the gospel you talked about. But now I'm in a hurry. I must go to the Master; he needs help from a physician. I think we should meet again later. Peace be with you!" He hugged me rapidly and disappeared like the others among the trees. I felt terribly baffled, and a crystal clear laugh from Lydia didn't make it any better.

The atmosphere in the herb garden was starting to get as dark as the nightfall, which slowly crept in between the blue-shimmering leaves of the olive trees. A man detached himself from the shadows of the fig trees that I passed. I had never seen him before. I had intended to leave the famous herb garden before dark. Lydia was now walking at my side and we were chatting. The man stood in my way.

"Tell me who you are," he asked me. "There is a rumor here that you are an Angel. It cannot be true. Angels don't walk on the ground dressed in a monk's habit. And who is that woman at your side? If you are Roman spies you will soon find yourselves alone in this garden. We can disappear very quickly. You won't catch any of us, understand?"

"I really don't want to." I gave him a friendly smile. "My name is Jan, and I'm a friend of your Savior, even if I live in another place. Peace be with you, brother! What is your name?"

"Judas Iscariot. Tell me why you and that woman walk around here?

What do you want from us, we poor disciples of the greatest Teacher of all. We are assembled here on the third day after the Crucifixion to comfort each other in our grief."

"This woman is my companion, Lydia, and she came with me to Earth. We are Angels who seek the Truth."

"Angels have haloes, and they don't appear to ordinary people," Judas objected. "I don't know what kind of Truth you are rambling on about. The Master is the Truth, and he doesn't exist anymore."

"He exists, and you will meet him soon. Do you believe us now?" Lydia lifted her arms and suddenly she had a radiant halo of light around her. My magic companion, I thought cheerfully.

Judas looked devastated. He put his arm over his eyes and recoiled to protect himself. Lydia stood there radiating all she could, but Judas took to his heels. He was very afraid of us Angels, even though he was a disciple of Christ!

15. The Revelation –
Paul Meets Jesus and Finds Salvation

"I've had enough of disciples," Lydia declared, and she pulled me towards the exit of the garden. No human being was in sight anymore. It was as if everybody had escaped from the "horrifying Angels." This was the first time in my angel-life I have ever scared people, and Lydia and I had a good laugh.

"You must meet Paul, too," Lydia decided. "He persecuted Jesus and his disciples long before the Revelation. Sit down and I will transport us!" She put her hands over my eyes and I felt something move. I don't know how; I only know that when I opened my eyes I was sitting on a piece of rock, close to a country road. I stroked my forehead. At first everything seemed to be shrouded in mist. When it cleared I discovered it was very hot and that I had a clear view of those who walked on the road. Suddenly I saw Jesus walking along the road. I didn't recognize him as a transparent Spirit, yet I questioned his condition. He had been ill since the Crucifixion and he looked pale and frail. Could he really have come all the way from Carmel? This must be some kind of projection, a hologram.

I had been brought directly to the meeting between Paul and Jesus. I would probably be a passive viewer and listener at this meeting. The Bible tells us that Jesus appeared in a bright light when he met Paul. At first I didn't see any light, except for the Sun, but that was about to change very soon. I was sitting behind a very large old tree. Jesus stopped right in front of the tree and I saw Paul coming from the other direction. He stopped when he saw Jesus. Then I discovered that the Master seemed luminous. Maybe it was magic? Well, in that moment it was certainly necessary, I thought.

"Who are you?" stammered Paul. He was a tall and lean man, slightly bent, grizzled, and with a long beard. His dark eyes burned. I didn't like his energies. He made a brutal and arrogant impression on me. I was sitting thinking about his perception of women and felt not at all happy. But when Jesus started radiating light Paul fell on his knees on the gravel and put his hands over his face. His mouth, or what I could see of it in his bushy beard, was babbling something.

Jesus bent forward and touched Paul. The man looked up at him, and then Jesus put one hand on his forehead and one on his crown. "I'm Jesus, and I have come to save you. You need to dedicate yourself to my wisdom and help me preach it to the people. You must be my disciple, dear Paul!, and you must talk about Love instead of revenge."

The man who rose laboriously with his hands folded in prayer was not the same arrogant figure who had come down the road. Tears were streaming down the bearded cheeks and I saw that his legs were shaking. I wondered inside how a man with feelings of such strong hatred against the disciples of Jesus could turn into a Christian preacher in just a couple of minutes, but that is what happened. I don't think that it was only the luminous Revelation; I believe it was a kind of interpenetration into the soul of Paul. Something in Jesus melted the resistance of the coming disciple. It was a strange sight to behold.

"Walk in peace to Damascus," said Jesus. "When you arrive there you must look for my disciple Ananias and receive the Baptism. After that you will return to Jerusalem. There you will be informed how to preach my teaching in the best way."

I stretched out my neck until it hurt. I thought that Paul behaved like a sleepwalker or as if he was hypnotized. Jesus disappeared as quickly as he had arrived. Paul continued his walk as if he was in a trance. I really hoped it was an unconscious hypnosis from the Master, because if not, he would have been illegally trespassing into the soul of Paul. The freedom of man must not be violated, because it is inviolable. When I thought of the Bible I remembered that hypnotism often intrudes upon freedom of thought. But anyhow, the Bible is not my guiding principle.

"Angel Jan, have you finished looking?" Jesus stood there, behind the tree and in front of me. He had disappeared from Paul's sight. For a second I saw a twinkle in his eyes. He asked me what I thought of the swift change of Paul. I decided to be honest.

"I hope he didn't change against his inner will," I said. "You cannot be converted that quickly without hypnotic influence."

"I will see you in Heliopolis!" Jesus answered, and I understood that his substitute body couldn't last very much longer.

Of course I would visit him in Egypt. I replied loudly to him and I heard Lydia's giggling voice, "Of course you will go there eventually."

It was a swift event I had witnessed, but it had made a strong impression on me. I wished I had Mary Magdalene beside me. She must know if her husband manipulated people.

Lydia read my thoughts. "Now you are a terrible skeptic," she shouted, fully visible sitting on the cliff beside me. "Contemplate why you have these thoughts!"

"Well, it's Paul," I answered. "How can such a cruel person be changed in one minute? He participated in the stoning of Stephen, he was allowed to persecute Jesus' disciples even outside Palestine, he was the cause of several cruel murders. Pious is not a word that suited him – then. Afterwards he became the darling boy of popes and bishops. What's behind all this?"

"Nobody has told you about his disastrous marriage to a very dominating wife and only one child, who was born a cripple and who died in pain after a couple of years," Lydia told me. "His wife was Christian and tried to convert him. This resulted in an enormous hatred in Paul. In fact, he hated his wife. He started to persecute Christians, and nobody could imagine that in the future he would be an ardent champion of the Christian faith. That is what happened, and it happened right here, on the road to Damascus." In that respect the Bible is correct.

"Really," I sighed. "There are always explanations of why people become this or that …" I was about to say something more when I felt Lydia's hands around my head, and everything disappeared.

16. The Resurrection – A Diversion

"I have been pondering about something, Kualli," I said. "The Resurrection is one of the keystones of Christianity, but what really happened? According to all existing sources, the disciples saw Jesus disappear into a light. Was it Christ who resurrected and Jesus who remained on Earth?"

"No. Christ returned to his Father and Creator when Jesus sank into a coma and when everybody thought he was dead. I can see it is time to make a peep-hole to the Resurrection, in order for you to draw your own conclusions.

"Lydia will go with you, and both of you will stay invisible on this visit into the secrets of time. I assure you that it's about time now to reveal a great secret!"

Lydia took my hand and the peep-hole opened. We were standing on the top of a mountain. There was a beautiful sunset. The Sun was sinking down and the first rose-colored gleam was changing to a deeper red and orange, mixed with a lovely golden light. It was so beautiful that I forgot everything else. Everything was rose-colored, the gray mountain with its deep-green moss seemed like a sea of roses, and the bushes and the few small flowers glittered in variant rosy hues. Lydia pinched my arm and I jumped and yelled – but no one saw us. Now, at last, I became aware of the scenery in front of us.

I counted fifteen people sitting in a semi-circle on the ground. They were all facing the slowly sinking Sun. There were a couple of women among them; I recognized Mary from Bethany and her sister Martha. Jesus was standing before them. We saw his silhouette outlined against the gold-red background. He gave each of them advice about the work he expected them to perform in the future when he had disappeared. He exhorted them to carefully listen inwards, to their hearts, to their innermost consciousness, and experience his participation from there. He wished them also to teach people to listen to their inner voice. We all have God's voice inside of us if we only are able to listen, he explained.

After that he exhorted them sternly not to break the semicircle and leave the mountain until the absolute right moment had appeared. If they did, they would break the cosmic harmony, which must not happen, because now they were going to experience the Holy Spirit. He didn't tell them how, he just asked them to stand up. They all crossed their arms over their breasts, like the Essenes. Then he turned and went to the edge of the mountain, where the red light from the Sun was changing to shadows and the Sun was disappearing like a glittering ball, thrown by Angels' hands. Right there he raised his hands to heaven and started to pray.

He was surrounded by radiance and then he was enveloped by a haze. After a while this mist-like haze elevated and raised upwards. Jesus was gone. I could also see a faint light where he had been standing. It darkened and someone cried that they could now leave the mountain. Another voice answered that they had been ordered to wait for the arrival of the Holy Spirit.

In the descending dusk I could see Lydia looking at me and putting a finger on her mouth. I noticed a glimpse of merriment in her eyes. I couldn't see anything funny in what I had seen; I found it serious and incomprehensible. But Lydia was Lydia.

It was not long before a new light appeared at the spot where Jesus had disappeared. I could vaguely discern two figures in the light. They were talking to the disciples – at least I heard voices asking them to receive the Holy Spirit and the Word and to teach the Laws of Heaven. After that, these figures disappeared as fast as they had emerged. I pinched myself in my invisible arm. This really seemed like magic.

"Gosh!" I was amazed. "Have I witnessed a real miracle?"

"You could say that," Lydia answered, and I could see her smile in the dark. "This peep-hole is unique. But now we will start looking further down the mountain on the other side."

"Looking?" I protested. "You can see nothing in this darkness."

"The darkness was necessary," answered Lydia, and she pulled me towards the edge of the mountain. I had been expecting a precipice but actually there was a road, or more exactly, an animal path leading down the other side. I noticed that not only were we invisible and could sail through the air, but also that we could just about see in the increasing darkness. Quite far below us I saw two torches. Lydia hurried in front of me and I had to follow.

To my great astonishment I saw Jesus and another dark figure walking below us. They walked swiftly with the torches as their only guiding light. They walked with their feet on the ground, small stones got rolling, and we could hear pebbles being crunched underfoot. There was no doubt that the faintly visible silhouettes in front of us were human beings. Besides, it was impossible not to recognize Jesus. His carriage and his special manner of walking was something I already had noticed. Yet, I was really surprised. How did he do that?

Lydia didn't stop until both figures had disappeared into a cottage just beneath the mountain. Jesus stopped, too, and looked around in both directions. Then I was able to verify that it really was Jesus. He and the other person went through the small door and I heard it slam loudly.

A big fig tree stood very near the cottage. We sat down for a while under its friendly leaves. I had to know what was happening. Was it sorcery or could it be explained physically?

Lydia took both my hands and squeezed them hard. "Calm down, Jan; you will get your explanation," she said. "In Tibet, India, and Egypt the great Masters can create substitute bodies (or holograms) by the use of projection. Jesus learned that from those Masters. If you want to disappear, you create a substitute body, and then you quickly get out of view. Surely it's magic, but many wise Masters know how to do it, because it is an ancient art that has also been used for defense. I cannot tell you how to do it, but when you know how, it is not very difficult. The procedure is a well-kept secret. In this case, I suspect Jesus found it necessary because he wanted to show that his God-Spirit had returned to its origin."

"You know what?" I was angry now. "I call that fraud. Pure cheating. It's got nothing to do with the Truth."

"Hasn't it?" Lydia asked mildly. "You have just gotten to witness the Truth. You don't have to tell everybody the Truth. Those who are supposed to get it will have it. It's all so wisely arranged."

"But this is going to be published in a book," I snorted. I was still angry. "Then everybody will get the Truth. And please tell me, who were these two suspicious individuals who called themselves the Holy Spirit?"

"Oh, I'm sure it was Jesus and his friend," Lydia answered, laughing happily. "I think it was done well. At that time everybody was very superstitious, and that goes for the disciples too. They needed a large dose of strict admonitions and advice to keep going. Jesus was good at creating substitute bodies of different kinds, and at the moment of sunset he was helped by the dew.

"You heard how Jesus told the disciples that he intended to appear physically to them again. That was a great consolation to them, because they thought he was dead. But if he really was dead it would be difficult to explain his repeated returns afterwards. But Jan, he really had what you call supernatural gifts. He could relocate from one place to another, making it appear physical when in fact it wasn't. Many Eastern wise men have succeeded in appearing at different places at the same time. That's possible to perform."

"So, the whole Resurrection is a bluff?" I snorted again. I couldn't swallow all I had heard.

"More of a diversion," Lydia answered. "And what you are saying about this being published in a book doesn't really matter. Those who are supposed to know will know. It's as simple as that. Hush, someone is coming."

The door of the cottage opened, and in the faint light from within I recognized the tall man who was Jesus' companion. It was his brother, Joseph of Arimathea. Jesus was standing behind him.

"You'd better stay here for a couple of days," said the merchant. "Nobody will look for you. This is my cottage, and it is believed to be uninhabited. I use it as a store of goods. You will find plenty of food and water here, and tomorrow I will send a reliable person who can help you and keep you company until it's time for you to go to Egypt. Remember, you promised to show yourself to your disciples a couple of times. If you need to contact me, tell the man who comes tomorrow."

"I feel guilty," said Jesus, rubbing his brow. "I feel as if I have deceived my friends and disciples."

"No, don't regret anything," Joseph admonished. "You would have been killed if they had gotten hold of you. You don't know who you can trust. It only takes one idle word. You must get out of this country as soon as possible. Until then, you are perfectly safe here. Peace be with you, beloved brother." He hugged Jesus and disappeared into the dark night.

"The Crucifixion has become an absurd drama," I muttered. "The symbol of the cross is just a stage prop."

"Now, listen to me before we go back," asked Lydia. "Amenhotep the Fourth, who was a unique pharaoh in Egypt and who prayed to the Sun instead of to the false gods, used the cross as a symbol in his mystery school. If a person stands with his arms outstretched at sunrise, a shadow appears on the ground, in the form of a cross. At that time this was a common greeting. When the person moves, the shadow disappears. This means that the temporary shadow is a symbol of the physical body and existence of man.

"Later on a rose was put on the cross. The rose was an image representing the human soul, through its transformation from a bud into a flower. The rose and the cross together represent the evolution of soul through human physical experience. Sometimes Jesus was called 'The Rose.' The rose came to represent Jesus' soul on the cross. In Egypt, a circle eventually was added on top of the cross, meaning 'eternal life.' It's called the Ankh-cross. Many centuries later, the church fathers put a crucified body on the cross as a symbol for Christianity. Jesus would not have liked that."

I looked at the cottage next to us. I saw a faint light coming from it, and we took the liberty of peeping inside through the small window without any glass. We were invisible, weren't we? I felt slightly like this was a violation of domicile, but I was too curious. We saw Jesus praying. He emitted a faint light, perhaps his halo. There was a jar and a half-eaten piece of bread on the table. We saw a bench in the corner with soft cushions and a thick blanket. In another corner there was a cupboard. In an open fireplace the remains of a fire were still glowing. I grabbed Lydia's arm and she turned a smiling face to me.

"I don't like this," I whispered. "Let's go home. I have a feeling that 'our friend in there' knows about us."

At that moment Jesus stood up and went to the window. "If there are any Angels around this house, I thank you," he said.

I fled in panic, but Lydia slowly left the place. "Calm down, Jan, we'll go home now!" she shouted.

We did. But this time I had the feeling of having made a forbidden journey. I felt like a child who had spied on his parents. At the same time, it had been great to experience the Resurrection. I had very mixed feelings running through me. But I will never again call what I saw "sorcery." It was a magic experience, created by a very great Master.

17. Luke, Who Nursed Jesus After the Crucifixion

"Actually, I got curious about that man Luke," was the first thing I said when I met Kualli again. "He pretended to agree with all I said, and actually he very well knew that Jesus was alive. What a scoundrel!"

"He was afraid to betray his friend Jesus," Kualli answered. "He was the one who helped to nurse Jesus right after the Crucifixion. The Master was hidden in Bethany, in a house of friends near his mother's dwelling. Luke and Mother Mary watched over him every night and nursed him with healing herbs and ointments. They couldn't take him to Carmel until his wounds were healed and he was feeling better. If you want to visit Luke, we can do that later. He also wrote the Acts of the Apostles when he was quite old."

"Please give me a peep-hole to some kind of in-between time, I asked. "What happened to him? There are so many different tales about him. Some say he was an artist, a painter. Was he a close friend of Paul?"

"He painted and wrote," answered Kualli. "All right then, Luke followed Paul on some journeys, including to Rome, and off to Rome you go!"

Off we went, me and my lovely companion. We ended up in a city, and it was definitely Rome. The Coliseum stood as a giant roundel in an area that was once a swamp, which had dried out. The old amphitheater must be over 100 years old. I wondered, how on Earth could we find Luke in this huge place?

As usual, Lydia answered my thoughts. We were both visible, and Lydia was wearing a pink dress with a light-gray shawl. "We were not sent here at random, Jan," she said. "We are going to meet Luke right here, and there he is!"

I stared in surprise at two men in Roman clothes walking slowly towards us. This time Luke seemed more mature. His tall, lean figure was dressed in a yellow robe with a loose fitting cloak in the same color. His brown hair was now grizzled and thin on top. Paul walked at his side, and they seemed to be having an amusing conversation. When Luke saw us he immediately stopped.

"Angel Jan!" he exclaimed. "I remembered we arranged to meet again, but I didn't think it would take this long. This is my friend Paul. We are on a missionary journey. Please, come with us to our lodgings. Paul owns a house, and there is a nice eatery nearby. You must be hungry after the trip." His last words were meant as a joke, and I laughed. Luke patted my shoulder in a friendly way and bowed to Lydia, but Paul eyed her suspiciously.

"Have you written your gospel yet?" I asked when we were sitting at the long wooden table outside the eatery. Paul avoided sitting near Lydia, so she was sitting between Luke and me.

"I'm working on it now," Luke answered. "Why are you here, and what do you want to know?"

"Jesus is in Heliopolis, in the monastery," I said. "You must know that, don't you?"

"I have been there," Luke said. He was delighted when he saw my startled face. "Our mission continues, and I need inspiration from a higher source. In a way, our Master still leads us, at least a few of us. We are a small group that sometimes meets in Heliopolis. It includes Paul and me and John, Simon Peter, Nicodemus, and a few others. Thomas nowadays lives in Kashmir, but we write to one another."

"In the Acts of the Apostles, which you are going to write, you speak at great length about the Resurrection of Jesus," I said. "Yet you know that he is still alive on Earth. Why is that?"

"It was necessary for everybody to think that he was dead, Jan. The Romans in Jerusalem are very clever at finding people and threatening and torturing them if they think they can gain some knowledge. By the staging of the Resurrection, Jesus could be calm and not risk his life. Nobody believed he was still alive, and that's why I pretended to accept what you said in Gethsemane."

"What are you and Paul doing in Rome?" I asked. "Have you succeeded in converting any Romans?"

"Oh yes, a lot of them." Paul was the one who answered. "We have a small Christian congregation who assemble at my house. I am a kind of prisoner here in Rome; I'm under supervision. But I'm going to be preaching the words of Jesus for as long as I can."

"I'm just leaving," Luke said. "Jan talks about something he calls the Acts of the Apostles. I like writing, and perhaps it will result in something more than the story about our Savior. Paul has established one of the first Christian congregations in Philippi in Macedonia. I'm going there. Would you like to accompany me?"

I looked at Lydia. She shook her head with a smile, so I declined the offer.

"Have you abandoned your work as a physician?" I asked Luke.

"No, I help as many people as I can," he answered, "and at the same time I preach the teachings of Jesus. He has taught me ancient knowledge in the art of healing. There are sick people everywhere, and there's great need for help from travelling doctors. If you also can make people understand that the root of disease is in themselves, you have succeeded in more than one sense. Humans' thoughts are the most important thing of all. How I can help them, you might ask? The sick people are eager to recover. If they understand that their thoughts and their life-styles are contributing to their diseases, the will for change and the will for self-help will emerge. That's why I travel around. Jesus and Paul are my masters."

"Are you not married, Luke?" Lydia asked.

"That's the ultimate reason why I travel." Luke was very serious. "I married when I was young, and my wife was an infatuating girl. I loved her passionately, I was crazy about her. She died giving birth to our child, who died too. Being a doctor, I felt a terrible powerlessness. My grief was enormous. I try every day, all the time, to drown that grief through writing and travelling."

The Roman twilight was already falling as we consumed a delicious soup in the little eatery. There's something special about a Roman night.

The darkness is not impenetrable like it is in the northern countries. It falls like crystal glass, full of pure, ringing tunes. It is indigo, not black. On a starlit night like this there was enchantment in the air, which both Lydia and I felt. The crystal glass contained a great secret, a deep resonance in our hearts. It was time to go home.

I woke up in the Angelic Realm. The transitions were swift, but now I was used to that. Another thing I've gotten used to is the laughing face of Kualli at my bedside.

"Well," he said, "is it a bit clearer now?"

"Well, yes," I answered, "but I'm still a bit confused. Sometimes it makes sense, sometimes it doesn't."

"Listen, Jan! It is because it took 300 years for Christianity to be documented in the Bible with the truths that suited the bishops and Emperor Constantine. Now please rest for a while before I send you on the journey with Mary Magdalene. In Jerusalem, people knew that she could heal and that she was close to Jesus, but not everybody knew that they were man and wife. Therefore the Romans assumed that they lived in sin, which made them even more vulnerable.

If Mary Magdalene had been accessible after the Crucifixion she no doubt would have been disposed of, probably stoned. Obviously, Jesus knew this very well. However, the bishops and Constantine the Great didn't think that far. They made her into a whore because it made a good story and also made her contemptible. It was an outermost wizardly addition to the belittlement of women."

"And where did Paul, who didn't like women, go after Rome?" I asked. "He was not very keen on Lydia."

"He did a good job for the first Christians. He was a learned Man, even if he started as a tent-maker. His industriousness, stubbornness, and charisma made him a leader of the Christian congregation. Shortly after you met him he died as a martyr in Rome."

"What did Luke say about that? He left Paul the day after we did."

"Of course he mourned his old friend. He left for Philippi on the request of Paul. Therefore, it took a long time before he got to know what had happened to him. However, he finished his gospel and also started to write the Acts of the Apostles a couple of years after that. He was always travelling, always on the move."

"That's good to know," I muttered, just before my eyes closed and I fell asleep like a child. Because I was materialized on some of my peephole journeys, I felt human fatigue. Or perhaps I needed sleep because of the very strange journey I was about to experience.

18. The Adventurous Voyage with Mary Magdalene

It was like a film, cut and directed by the great Director of Heaven. This time I woke up in the middle of a caravan destined for Joppe. I was sitting on a donkey, which I didn't appreciate. I resentfully realized that my mission involved a certain amount of discomfort. My legs were too long for hardships like this; I felt like a daddy-longlegs trying to climb a curtain.

"How are you, Jan!" A fully visible Lydia was riding on the donkey in front of me. I kicked with my heels on the sides of my means of transport, to move it forward. The donkey turned her head and looked at me with big, hurt eyes. Instead of hurrying forwards she slowed down. Lydia laughed at me as usual and rode to my side. I saw Mary Magdalene further along the road. She was leaning forward, eagerly talking to a man on a donkey at her side. He carried her little son on his saddle. I asked Lydia who he was.

"It's Nicodemus," she answered. "He is also one of Jesus' disciples. He is very learned and very devoted to Jesus. Mary Magdalene has the chalice, Jan, the very famous Grail! It is going further on to Britain, and Nicodemus has the mission to take it there."

"Is it going to Glastonbury?" I asked. I was impressed that I was taking part in such great and secret historic events. Lydia nodded and put a finger to her mouth.

I'd better be silent; I was a little too curious, I thought. Concurrently I remembered how moving the goodbye had been between Jesus and Mary Magdalene. I could hear her sob, "When are you coming to fetch me?" And I could also hear Jesus' evasive but loving answer. Mary Magdalene should be kept from knowing about the Crucifixion, but I think she guessed that something terrible was in store for her husband. Jesus had told that he would be imprisoned and that could only mean one thing.

I was happy to have Lydia with me. I was no good at comforting women. I wondered if Jesus and his wife really would be reunited again, since he didn't die on the cross. If this was the Truth, I hoped it would be hopeful for both parties. But now I had no time to ponder any more. The air was full of the scents that characterize the sea: salt, seaweed, and lovely fresh winds. We had arrived in Joppe, and our ship was waiting at the quay.

It was a big cargo ship, well-built and stable and with all sails set. We jumped off our donkeys and started to unload. Well, I can't say I jumped from my donkey. To be honest, that terrible animal shook elegantly and I fell – less elegantly. It was all very ignominious. My cloak entangled itself in something on the donkey. Lydia was holding her hands over her mouth and her shoulders were shaking and I understood very well why. An open monk's habit … I hurried to cover what was needed to be covered. I was the last one of a quite small group of people to walk up the gangway. After me they took the gangplank up and I was happy to see my donkey leaving the bay.

Our first port of call would be Ephesus. I had better get acquainted with the other passengers, because the journey would take several weeks. Nicodemus was a strange person. He was a Pharisee, versed in the Scriptures, and he had been a member of the Council. He had visited Jesus at night to get the education he desired. He was deeply engaged in the teachings of Jesus, something he had to hide from the other Jews. He really lived a double life, I thought, and he wanted to escape Jerusalem. A journey was a good excuse. Of course, nobody knew the real object of his journey.

Even in Biblical times, the Holy Grail was a hot potato! The story that had been woven about it in the last two thousand years was rather wrong. When I lived on Earth it was believed that the blood of Jesus had been collected in the Grail. I find that rather disgusting. And how would that be possible when soldiers were posted near the cross and nobody was allowed to be near it until the Master's body was fetched by Joseph of Arimathea? And, in case that it happened, who took care of the blood, and why? As you know, blood dries. Mary his mother and Mary from Bethany were chased away from the cross at an early stage, and so was John the Beloved. However, it is possible that somebody spread a lie about all this, but it was Mary Magdalene who kept the Grail all the time. Jesus had neither time nor frame of mind for physical objects.

"Are you really an Angel? Then, why are you with us on this trip?" Nicodemus asked me with smiling eyes. He was a tall man with a well-built, muscular body. His eyes were blue-gray, sharp and observant. He had a big nose and a friendly, generous mouth. His hair and beard were dark brown. Some silvery hairs shone among the dark-brown. He seemed to be about forty-five.

"Yes, I'm an Angel, and I've got the mission of accompanying Mary Magdalene to Gaul," I answered. "I know you are going further on to Britain, aren't you?"

Nicodemus nodded. "Maybe we can go together?" he suggested with a happy smile. "It wouldn't hurt having an Angel with me on that trip. It could be pretty adventurous, if you like adventures."

"I'll sleep on that and ask in the higher Realms," I answered. It could be really interesting to go to the future home of the Grail. I'm very curious about the Holy Grail."

"I'm going to preach a little over there," he confided in me. "What I learned from the Master is worth spreading to a bigger audience. Regarding the Grail, my friend, it's not holy, but it has a symbolic meaning."

We talked a lot during the journey and soon became very good friends. I also liked Mary Magdalene a lot. She brought a young woman, called Hanna, with her. Hanna was a nurse and helped her with the boy. The child she would give birth to was expected to come after the arrival in Gaul. Hanna was young and pretty, with merry eyes. She radiated joie de vivre and really seemed to enjoy this trip. Her hair was as black as Mary Magdalene's was red. Mary had also brought an Arab man, who seemed to be some kind of servant. He was called "the Arab." He was giant-size and full of power and strength. I later learned that he was a faithful old servant who had been with her since childhood.

There was also a young man, called Benjamin. He was a friend of the apostle John the Beloved, who sent him to accompany Nicodemus. The long trip to Britain would be too dangerous to make alone. I felt very inclined to go with them, but first we had to arrive in Gaul.

There was also an elderly couple on the boat, who I really couldn't identify. They kept to themselves and seemed very fond of each other. Both looked very nice and seemed kind and enjoyable. We only exchanged a couple of words now and then. The man had short white hair, thinning on top. He had a big nose and thin lips and looked very Jewish. The woman was more difficult to identify. She was plump, with a nice face, big dark eyes, and a generous mouth. Little David liked her very much; she played with him and relieved Mary and Hanna now and then.

I don't intend to tire out the reader with a detailed description of the journey on the boat, but I will tell you a couple of important things that happened during the trip.

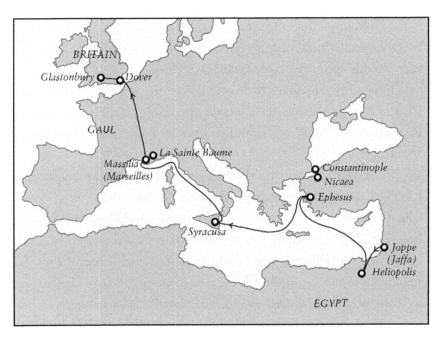

Mary Magdalene's journey to Gaul and the Grail's journey to Britain.
La Sainte Baume is said to be the place where Mary Magdalene lived.

We arrived at the harbor in Ephesus after a dreary storm that kept us in the cargo-hold of the boat. There were only a few of us, but the captain told us that some more passengers would come aboard in Ephesus. There was not much room in the cargo-boats, but there were many of them sailing between Joppe and Rome. I don't know if my readers today can imagine what an active boat-traffic there was in those times! Even the Bible describes it as natural for people to travel, often and everywhere.

One of Jesus' disciples was called Maximin. He was born in the South of Gaul (current Provence). For reasons I don't know, he went to Jerusalem and ended up among the disciples. When Jesus was threatened by Kaifas, Maximin felt things were getting too hot for comfort and returned to his native country to preach what he had learned from Jesus. At that time many gods were worshipped in Gaul and he saw his mission to teach about the one and only God. Maximin was still a young fellow, 28–30 years old. On his way home he stayed in Ephesus in order to establish a Christian congregation, but this had failed. and now he was returning home to Gaul with our ship.

When the wind slackened and we came near to Ephesus, Benjamin told us that Maximin belonged to his own circle around Jesus. There were several circles, some older, some younger, some uneducated, some highly educated. About sixty men, among them also a few women, assembled every day around the Master or followed him on his wanderings. I listened to many interesting stories about these people, many destinies. We wondered how these disciples who were still alive would go on teaching, and we also wondered if Jesus was alive and where he was living. I could not tell them what I knew about the Master, because then I would interfere in history in an unallowable way. That was not my mission. I was a spectator looking for the Truth. I was only a link into Eternity.

We saw Ephesus lying like a daub of color, surrounded by blue water and blue sky. Then Lydia came to me. She had been out of sight for a few days. I knew she was with Mary Magdalene.

"Jan, please come and help me," she asked. When I looked at her I saw she was pale and had dark shadows under her eyes. "Mary's little son David is sick. He is in a very bad state. We must try to help him."

"You very well know we are not allowed to interfere physically," I answered, as I went with her to Mary and Hanna. Mary Magdalene had the little one on her lap. The child was breathing heavily and his cheeks were glowing red as if he had a high temperature. I persuaded Mary to leave her son to us, so that she could get a little rest. She had to remember the child in her belly. The unborn one would be influenced by fatigue, worry, and fear from its mother. At last she agreed, and she laid down on a soft piece of carpet, which Hanna had spread out beside us. I saw that Mary immediately fell asleep.

It won't be long now before we call at Ephesus, I thought. How nice to feel the ground beneath my feet, even if it is only for a few days. The ship would be repaired and get new cargo. We were to stay at an inn near the harbor. I felt quite tired, but decided to stay awake until we arrived. The captain had promised that there was only one more hour to go.

The little boy in my arms lay remarkably still. He was breathing hard and sort of gurgling. A thin fluid ran down his chin. His eyes were closed, but he was still breathing. I called for Lydia, because the boy must be seriously ill. The elderly couple were sitting nearby. They took the boy so that I could talk to the captain. The last thing I saw when I looked behind was that the elderly woman, who was called Mayah, had taken the boy in her arms. I couldn't see her husband. She slowly rocked the boy and kissed him tenderly, as if he were of her own family. That made an impression on me.

Nicodemus called on me. "I must talk to you about the boy," he said. "Little David is not dying. He is not even sick. They have given him an herb to make him sleep very deeply. Mayah and her husband are taking care of him and they are going to take him to an Essene monastery at Lake Garda (current north Italy). This was arranged long ago and Jesus knows about it, but he didn't want to inform Mary Magdalene. He knew how upset she would be. She would never leave the boy. I must tell her the truth when we have landed in Ephesus.

There is a price on David's head, and Rome has spies everywhere."

"Then she must get to know it now," I said angrily, "or she will go crazy!"

Nicodemus hesitated, and then he nodded. "You're right; it's better to do it now. You tell her, Jan. But the other passengers, except you, Lydia, and maybe the Arab, must believe that he has been abducted."

"In modern language, kidnapped," I snapped, and went straight to his sleeping mother. I really feared that she would have a miscarriage when she got this terrible news. Lydia and I told her the truth very carefully, and she took it surprisingly well. She confessed that she had suspected that something was going to happen to her son. She was angry that Jesus had not told her. I assured her she could visit her son in the monastery whenever she wished. I told her how necessary it was that he was abducted, but after that she sulked and didn't want to talk to either me or Nicodemus.

We arrived at Ephesus late at night. In spite of the late arrival, it still looked vivid and colorful in the lantern light. Mary Magdalene had a black shawl around her head and was leaning against Hanna. She had wanted to say farewell to her little son, but was not allowed by Nicodemus. Her tears were streaming continuously.

When finally the gangplank was laid down and we could start the landing procedure, Nicodemus and I helped her ashore. One moment she was in despair, the next she was furious. She leaned sometimes against me or Nicodemus, sometimes on Hanna or Lydia. The Arab was standing behind, looking very unhappy. No one had yet informed him about David, and he couldn't understand where the child was. He was going to be informed later, according to Nicodemus.

Lydia had a defense speech for Jesus. "What if your husband makes it over there in Jerusalem?" she said. "What if he survives? What would he say about your grief that could lead to a miscarriage? You can protect your unborn child in many ways, but not by grieving yourself to death. We, all your friends, understand your feelings, dear. You have lost David, even if it is not forever. You don't know if your husband is alive, if he makes the trial. But we also know that if your husband is not alive anymore, he will appear to you. He hasn't yet, so there is good hope that he's still alive. You will surely get a message eventually when we come to Gaul. Give him the opportunity of embracing at least one child!"

Lydia succeeded in pressing the most tender points of Mary and made her think clearer. Maximin greeted us as soon as we reached the inn. He and Benjamin fell in each other's arms, and Benjamin told as much as he could. Maximin seemed to be a very nice young man. He was clean-shaven, had black curly hair, and dark eyes. His face was beautiful and his body thin and lithe. Nicodemus seemed content to have yet another man in our company. We definitely had many hardships in front of us.

The elderly couple were not on the ship anymore. They had left the boat in Ephesus without saying goodbye to us. We couldn't see them in the crowded harbor, nor at the inn. It was as if the earth had swallowed them up. What a risk they ran, I thought, and I admired them for it.

19. The Boat Trip Continues from Ephesus to Massilia

We soon left Ephesus for the fair Sicily and Syracuse. The distance was about the same as from Joppe to Ephesus, and I was worried about Mary Magdalene. Would she manage this long trip without a miscarriage? Long journeys at sea can cause both dreams and nightmares. I had some indefinable feeling that I was on this trip solely to help her regain her security and balance. I needn't have worried.

Mary Magdalene was strong – I have never seen a stronger woman! After the pause in Ephesus she seemed to trust the future, and her devotion to and love of God had not changed, but had become perhaps stronger. I saw her pray several times a day. We joined in her prayers morning and evening. Our captain, who was a robust, bearded man in his fifties, worshipped her. When he looked at her, his hard, marine-seasoned face became as soft as a child's, and he took part in our prayers as often as he could.

I was formidably curious about the Grail, but Mary kept it hidden somewhere in her luggage or perhaps in her loose clothes. I really found this time at sea went faster than the previous one. Perhaps I had gotten used to it, perhaps it was because of our strong companionship that felt so good. Angels don't accept time the same way as humans, so I don't know how long the trip was.

Lydia was a considerable help. Hanna fell seasick and was actually feeling bad all the time. Lydia had a way of encouraging people that was rather unusual. She told such unbelievably scary stories that you didn't know whether to laugh or be terrified.

I had many interesting talks with Mary Magdalene. Often we sat on deck in the twilight when the weather was nice. I think it was good for her to talk about things that interested us both, especially Jesus, of course. On one occasion I asked her if it was true, as it says in the Bible, that Jesus had driven seven demons out of her. I could never imagine this wonderful woman having to deal with these terrifying things. A ringing laughter was the answer.

"There were no demons," she assured me. "I believe Peter started that rumor. Sometimes the Apostles were jealous, and that was a problem for me. Do you know what my husband actually did? We were already married at that point. He opened my seven chakras and cleaned them. Every human ought to do that from time to time if their chakras are not already open. Jesus had learned that in India. Maybe the Apostles only heard the number seven and assumed that it was demons." She laughed again and I understood she was telling the truth.

"There are many stories about the woman who anointed Jesus with an expensive oil, which angered the disciples. Was that you?"

"Yes, of course it was me. I lived in Bethany then, waiting for my husband to come home from one of his journeys. Martha, Mary, and Lazarus were my old friends. You know how we met. Jesus was a good friend of the Bethany family and he went to Bethany right after the Baptism. His mother, who was a widow, had a cottage nearby, where he often stayed."

"The Bible only mentions one anointing woman. Why weren't you named?"

"Because I was a woman. The disciples did not like that entire occurrence at all. I could afford to buy that kind of oil, and because Jesus and I were married, they should not have interfered." I was to learn more about that anointing later on.

We had quite good weather on the way to Syracuse, and I believe we reached the harbor in very reasonable time. The harbor was as colorful as Ephesus, but there was something I had missed for a long time: music. The local people played and sang, and we listened happily to all these new melodies, some caressing and some wild, that we heard the few days we stayed there. The inn was dirty and crowded, but the atmosphere was wonderful. There were lots of heathens and fleas, but only nice ones! We sang and danced and drank the excellent wine. I don't remember that many more details of that harbor! Here it was Nicodemus who held the reins, and we stuck to him.

When we left Syracuse, the atmosphere on board was also good. The ladies had bought new dresses and other things that women like, and the men had also invested in some favorite things. I had to wear that monk's habit the whole time, but I bought some new things to wear underneath it! Lydia, who preferred to be visible on the whole trip, had bought a dress of sea-green silk and an embroidered, glittering shawl. I wondered where she had gotten the money, but I didn't ask.

Nicodemus played the gentleman host. He seemed to have a lot of money. I suspected that Mary Magdalene had given the ladies their accessories. She was a wealthy woman and had probably brought some money with her, considering the hardships we could encounter.

The next harbor was the last one. It was Massilia (current Marseille) in Gaul. It was not far away now, and that was good. We all were worn out by the eternal sea. I was getting increasingly concerned about Mary, although she was still dashing. Her belly was very big and she walked the deck like a duck in peril at sea. But Mary had a good sense of humor. She patted herself on the belly and asked the baby boy – she was certain it was a boy – to wait until we came ashore. And the baby might have heard her – but couldn't wait a second longer!

The first thing I saw when the ship was gliding into the harbor of Massilia was a line of tents along the beach. We reefed the sails and had a good wind for the short distance towards the quay. Then it started. I had no chance to look at the tents, because Mary Magdalene cried out loudly. Her labor had started. She was put on a primitive stretcher and she was the first one to be carried down the rapidly laid gangway. The rest of us, terrified, were crowded around her. Now and then there was a cry that made my blood run cold. Was everything all right?

A tall woman with a dark complexion made her way through the crowd. There was always a crowd when a cargo boat was expected. The woman was followed by many men and women with similar appearance. They were dressed in colorful clothes, and the tall woman wore lots of jingling jewelry. The crowd made way for her and saluted her reverently.

"It is Sarah, the Black Queen," our captain shouted to us, and leaned over the rail and waved to her. She waved back, and before we had a chance to react, her men had taken the stretcher with Mary Magdalene. They ran towards the beach and the tents I had observed from the boat. Of course we went with them.

Later I was informed that Mary was brought to the queen's own tent. When we arrived we were astonished by the magnificence and comfort inside the tents. On the walls, as well as on the floor, were beautiful carpets. Lustrous incense-lamps hung from the ceiling. There were brightly colored cushions to sit upon everywhere. One part of the tent was screened off with a curtain. That's where they took Mary. The queen, followed by Lydia and Hanna, showed us with a friendly gesture where to sit and wait.

The waiting was long, probably several hours. During that time we experienced a marvelous hospitality. Lovely young women in embroidered skirts and shirts served the most delicious food. They all had dark skin, black hair, and black eyes. I remembered that gypsies have their roots in northern India and that their tribe made them free from their original country and then they wandered around the world.

At last came the happy moment when the queen herself appeared and showed us the newborn baby, pretty as a picture, with thin red down on its head. It was a girl. Mary had had a troublesome delivery. Now everything was fine, except that she had hoped she would give birth to another son, a new little Savior.

The gypsies had all they needed in their tents. They were used to births and had a lot of herbs and homemade medicines and ointments that eased pain, cleaned, and healed. Now a group of men started to play on their strange stringed instruments. We watched dances and heard songs and music that welcomed the baby to Earth. I realized that Jesus had gotten a little daughter who surely would bring much joy to her parents. I hoped he would be told about this wonderful occasion, wherever he was, and I also hoped he would welcome a daughter as much as a son.

The gypsies offered us lodging and food until we had arranged our own. They were staying in Massilia a further short time. We were very grateful and accepted their offer. I was wondering where the Grail was now, and Nicodemus winked at me as if he had read my thoughts. It was probably safe in his custody. We were invited to go into the queen's private room to visit Mary Magdalene, who had the baby on her arm. The girl was called Sarah, after the Black Queen, who had been such a wonderful help. "Gaul feels welcoming," was my last thought before sleeping that memorable night in a tent where the men slept. The ladies were staying in another tent. I suspected Lydia to be here and there, because she was a prying soul. I laughed at the thought.

Already the following day, Mary walked with us along the shore, where long grass on the sandbanks marked the frontier to the settlements all around. We had to find somewhere to live, so we could start our own mission from there. Nicodemus didn't want to stay long with the gypsies. He was worried about the Grail among these wild, cheerful, foreign people. They couldn't presage what it represented.

I was anxious to get clear answers if I was allowed to follow Nicodemus on his imminent journey to Britain. It meant that I had to return to the Angelic Realm again, and Lydia told me she could arrange that. Nicodemus did not want to leave Mary Magdalene and the baby before they had found a house to live in. Maximin and Hanna would of course stay with her.

But terrible news reached us through the kind captain on the boat. He stayed for several days in the harbor because his boat had to be repaired. A ship arrived from Joppe and its captain told our captain about the Crucifixion. According to him, weird things had happened, but Jesus had died on the cross and had then been taken down and transferred to a relative's grave. This news came at the same time as we had found a suitable house up on a hill, with a lovely view over the little port. Lydia had to grasp me so that I didn't go straight to Mary Magdalene and tell her my version of the Crucifixion. I knew her husband was alive, and I couldn't tell her. Lydia calmed me and told me Mary surely would get to know the Truth soon. Jesus would undoubtedly send her a letter, but it felt terrible that we had to put in a good face and witness her new despair. First she had lost her little son David, and now she thought her husband was killed. I asked Lydia to arrange "the journey home." I was afraid I would prattle too much if I stayed and drank more of the delicious wine.

20. The Journey to Britain with the Grail

The journey home was swift, and I woke up as usual with Kualli sitting at my bed. This time he seemed to be in an enormously good mood. He was laughing. I frowned and was completely uncomprehending.

"Lydia has told me about your escapades, Jan!" he said. "You've managed quite well, and so far you have kept your mouth shut and withheld any forbidden knowledge. And you came back because you didn't want to be tempted to tell the Truth. But you are the one searching for the Truth!"

"I have come here to ask you if I may go with Nicodemus and Benjamin on their journey to Britain," I dryly remarked. "You mentioned nothing about it last time we were here, so I wanted to know if it is part of the plan."

"Initially it wasn't," said Kualli thoughtfully. "But we are fully prepared for the Truth to come up with new roads that need to be explored. Perhaps we should call it side roads, small paths in the forest of Truth. Of course you may go to Britain, my friend. There are many obscure sayings about the Grail; people have hyped it into something it actually isn't. That's why we also wish you to find out the Truth of the Grail. But you should know right from the start that the place where it is hidden must never be revealed to the public. You may not write about that. Just imagine how people would run and crowd that hideaway!"

"There is a book in the present time on Earth that describes exactly that, according to my medium," I said thoughtfully. "That book talks about the male and the female that the Grail represents. It refers to the womb of Mary Magdalene as the real Grail."

"So many ideas about the Grail have appeared through the centuries." Kualli smiled and his eyes seemed a little mischievous. "But shouldn't we after all believe the story that Jesus and Mary told us, that it is their wedding-chalice, representing yin and yang, but also eternity?"

"What do you mean by eternity?" I asked.

"Both drank out of it. Their alliance was eternal. Mary knew it, and you will notice she knows it when you meet her. She doesn't feel the pain any longer; she knows she is inseparably united with Jesus. That's why nobody else may have the Grail. It belongs to them, and only to them. Maybe you will find out more if you accompany Nicodemus. He is a sound man; he will never let you down. He is waiting for you now, so be off, my friend, be on your way."

Questions buzzed in my ears, but no answers came. I woke up in the house that Nicodemus had found for Mary Magdalene. She was standing at my bed, looking worried, with the sleeping baby in her arms.

"Dear Angel-friend," she said, caressing my front. "I'm so happy you are awake. You have been sleeping much too long and we couldn't wake you up. Lydia told us to wait, because you were far away and would soon return."

"I will accompany Nicodemus and Benjamin," I explained. "The Grail's journey will be my journey too."

"Good," Mary said, "because Nicodemus said he would leave as soon as you were back. He has found decent horses for you."

Oh yes, horses. There would be no motor vehicles in this century. I sighed and thought about all the hardships a horse trip could mean. If only there had been a wagon – but no. People walked or rode or went by boat. Boat to Britain would be too far. I had to just hang on. "But what about Lydia?" I asked.

"Lydia will go with you," answered Mary, and it was her turn to sigh. "I'm so fond of that woman. We think the same way about our Father and his works. I've succeeded in converting Sarah and her people here. She was the first one I baptized in Gaul, and that's why my daughter will be called Sarah. I feel such a great gratitude towards the queen, and as long as they stay here we are going to work together with the knowledge we have."

"You have to get the confidence of the people in Gaul, too," I said.

"It's here you are going to work for the next years. You speak their language and they seem to understand you."

Nicodemus showed me my proud courser. The horse was dapple-gray with a bushy mane and kind eyes. The other horses were brown. I dared to stroke the animal and gave him the good old Swedish horse-name Brunte.

It was hard to say goodbye to Mary Magdalene, and at the same time it felt good that she had Maximin as a protector when we left her. He seemed a little dreamy and romantic, but Nicodemus assured me that the boy could use his sword, if needed. The white house on the hill looked Roman, and it turned out that a Roman couple had built it. The husband had recently died and the Roman lady had returned home. Our captain recommended us warmly, and Nicodemus (or Mary Magdalene) bought the house at a fairly modest price.

Additionally, nearby were many other houses which turned out to belong to a colony of Jews who had settled in this place. Mary Magdalene was received with great joy in this Jewish colony, as were Nicodemus and Benjamin. It felt good, because these Jews were friendly people who enjoyed Massilia and who got along well with the rest of the population. I would have rather not left this oasis, but I hoped, anyhow, to come back fairly soon with good news.

We set off. Nicodemus had bought another horse for the luggage, and he also found out which roads to take and where to find the inns on our way. Benjamin seemed filled with knight-errantry, and his eyes were happy and expectant. We rode in silence. I had a tough job to get to know my horse and to handle it the right way. Lydia rode behind me. She seemed already to have mastered the art of riding, just as she mastered most things she did. She had a veil on as a precaution.

For someone who has never experienced a ride through Gaul (France), I warmly recommend such a horse trip. The beauty of the landscapes we passed was stunning; each of them smiled at us and welcomed us in different ways. We avoided the big roads (if there were any) and passed small idyllic villages, where we were received with great kindness. But Nicodemus was on his guard all the time, and we never slept all four at the same time. One of us always took the watch. There were robbers at this time, and the greatest benevolence at an inn could hide the biggest danger. But it all went well until we came to a place high up in the North of Gaul. We followed the river Rhone until we had to cross over to the other side of the river. Only certain villages had big rafts that could take both horses and their owners, but we found one and asked for a crossing. That would be possible early the next morning. I will never forget that morning!

Sunrise spread its lovely shimmer over the river. The day promised to be pleasant and warm. The raft had room for all four of us and the horses. Two big men from the village punted the raft, and the water was smooth as a mirror.

Once we had crossed the river we would just ride straight to the northwest towards the harbor, where the boat to Britain departed. It would take a couple of days, but we were delighted that our journey was about to come to an end. Perhaps we had a couple of weeks left of our journey. Mostly it depended on the weather. Heavy rain would delay us, but it was a good time of the year to be travelling in North Gaul.

It was a little tricky to get the horses ashore. They didn't like to be on the blue waves. To get ashore they had to wade a short distance in shallow water. The raft could not be docked as a normal boat. We mounted the unwilling animals and they splashed, neighing, through the water. As usual, Lydia rode after me. Suddenly I heard her cry out loudly. When I turned around I saw her horse had stumbled and her whole pack was in the water. Lydia was wet and I can assure you that she was very angry! She tore off her veil and behaved not at all Angelic. Then she squelched up on to land and Benjamin and I helped her with the horse and pack. I could hardly keep a straight face. It was now warm and sunny, and she dried quickly by a little fire we lit on the shore.

"It would have been more typical if it had happened to you," Lydia said, glaring at me. Then she started to laugh, long and heartily. Lydia was never gloomy for long; she had a very sunny temperament.

The raft was almost out of sight when we suddenly heard some strange noises from the bushes behind us. Near the shore was a thick, dense forest. The men on the raft had told us how to get through.

Nicodemus had risen and was about to lead the horses to us. Benjamin was putting out the fire and I was helping Lydia mount her horse when the misery broke loose. Robbers! Lots of robbers! We were easy prey for them. After a few minutes we were sitting on our horses, bound and gagged. Our journey was over, from all points of view. In that moment Nicodemus certainly must have thought that the Grail never would reach its destination. But neither had he counted on two Angels being a part of this trip.

"Hold on!" whispered Lydia in my brain. She was riding at my side, and I met her eyes. We had robbers in front of us, behind us, and at our sides. How would we get out of this? We had been told not to interfere in historical situations, but I soon learned that there are always exceptions.

"Come on," Lydia's voice said in my ear. When I looked at her again she had disappeared, and the robber at her side was staring, terrified, at her empty horse.

"Go ahead and put them to sleep!" Lydia whispered. "Both you and I know how to do it. Hurry up! I will take the right side and you take the left."

I obeyed the order. One by one I got the robbers on the left side to nod and fall asleep. Lydia loosened our knots as easily as if she had been a pupil of the famous Houdini. Nicodemus and Benjamin could see what we intended, and we galloped away at high speed in the direction that the men on the raft had shown us.

"They won't wake up for several hours," Lydia's voice assured in my ear, and she giggled happily. Sometimes it is good to be an Angel!

Nicodemus was in the front, and we rode for a long time through a landscape of cultivated fields. Apparently the robbers were located in the woods in the other direction. They lurked near the place where the raft came, in order to rob poor travelling people. We decided to report this in the nearest village.

We had no more major or dangerous incidents for the rest of the trip. We had to wait for a couple of days for the crossing to Britain, but it was really relaxing. We found a small inn with nice people and nice food. There we made jaunts along the beach and excursions in the mountains. It was a well-deserved rest after the tiresome ride through Gaul. My seat, despite my Angelic heritage, was the subject of quite painful soreness and scorch. It was lucky that Lydia was a good healer and wordlessly understood the origin of the pain.

21. The Holy Grail Gets Its Hiding Place

The first thing we saw in Britain was the cliffs of Dover (as they are called nowadays). It took a while to get to the mainland with the horses. I hadn't a clue where we actually were going, so now I thought it was time to ask. We rode for a while inland in the evening. When the shadows lengthened and a pale crescent moon could be discerned, we reached a small village with an inn. When we were sitting in the inn, sipping delicious English beer, I asked to know where we would bring the Grail.

"Well, we will continue further quite a long way," answered Nicodemus. "There is a remarkable place called Glastonbury in the county of Somerset. There we will meet an old friend. He knows all about the Grail and its remarkable power."

"Why could we not hide it in Jerusalem or in Egypt?" I asked.

"Well, that has something to do with the future," was the cryptic answer from Nicodemus. After that, he seemed unwilling to discuss it further. He changed the subject and told us about the country we were in right now and what went on there.

When we finally arrived at Glastonbury we were so tired and exhausted that the meeting with Joseph of Arimathea, the brother of Jesus, at first felt rather strained. He recognized me and seemed pleased with the composition of our company. He bowed reverently to Lydia when she was introduced as an Angel. Then he told us the true version of what had happened after the Crucifixion in Jerusalem, and Nicodemus and Benjamin were overjoyed. This was truly good news they would tell Mary Magdalene. Jesus was alive and was in the monastery of Carmel. His wounds from the Crucifixion were not yet healed, so he must rest and have treatment from skilled Essene monks there. It would certainly take several months before he was fully recovered. Joseph also knew that he thereafter planned to go to Egypt, to Alexandria and Heliopolis, under another name. There he would wait for Mary Magdalene and Sarah. Joseph would bring them there. Maybe they would be able to be together for a longer period. At least he hoped so. But this news was extremely secret. There was a price on the Master's head and he couldn't feel safe anywhere in the world under his own name.

The first evening we were together with Joseph, I was at last shown the Grail. It was made of alabaster that reflected all the colors of the spectrum on its even, golden surface. There were beautiful decorations on its foot, and on the upper part there were lovely jewels. I realized, however, that this was not an ordinary chalice – it was sort of luminous.

"When the hardest times in the history of the Earth are upon us, the Grail will be found," Nicodemus explained. "Then it will perform miracles. Its healing powers are extraordinary. But it must not fall into the wrong hands, and that's why we must hide it away very carefully. The secret is buried with us, and I presume the two Angels will keep it. However, you are obliged to save it if one day it is found by the wrong person."

"How can we know? Where will we be?" I muttered.

Nicodemus smiled, and Lydia looked furiously at me. Then I remembered that I was just an "occasional" human being. It is easy to fall too deep into character, I thought.

The next morning brought fog, but through the fog the sheerest sunlight was trying to penetrate its way down, and the air was fresh and cool when I met Lydia outside the inn.

"It's time," she said, smiling. "Now we will bury the Grail."

Joseph took us to a place that was so strange, that I shivered to the core of my soul. We first went up a high hill. There was a hollow tower at the top that you could enter. The tower was very ancient. (The Tor is said to be a remnant from the early Stone Age; see the picture on page 7.) The view from there was ravishing. At first I expected Joseph to bury the Grail up there, but I was wrong. He brought it out and raised it towards Heaven at the very moment the sun broke through the fog and started to glitter on the dew-wet grass. One ray fell directly on the Grail – and behold! It lit up like a lamp, and the light glowed not only inside it but also around it. It was as if it consumed light for the last time in a very long time. We fell on our knees and prayed, all five of us.

When we rose, we felt a peculiar atmosphere of Presence. The Grail shimmered, now somewhat weaker, but still so perfectly beautiful. We heard a swish, like a tone in the air. I cannot call it a song, just tones from the spheres. I noticed that Lydia reacted very strongly to the cosmic sounds. She took my hand and we stood there in quiet reverence. Our reverie was broken, however, when Joseph used his staff to show us to go ahead. I looked at his staff and wondered where he had gotten it. It looked like a branch from a tree. My Angel-memory told me that, according to an old tradition, Joseph of Arimathea planted his staff in the earth, where it rooted and started to grow. It existed in the form of a hawthorn tree when I lived on Earth (see the picture on page 9).

We went down the hill. I had a feeling as if we had left a pre-historic age, so dense and covered with so much mystery and dark shadows that I got goose pimples all over my arms, even though I was an Angel. I was filled with many questions that I wanted to ask Joseph of Arimathea. But now the solemn moment approached when the Grail would be positioned in its hiding place. Since I must not reveal where it was, I will only use the term "hiding place."

The famous well in Glastonbury is on a hill called Chalice Hill, and it runs down the hill in stairs, built of cobblestones. Every stair was an idyllic setting in itself, and all the way down we saw luxuriant vegetation with all kinds of flowers (see the picture on page 8). We walked around and listened to the rippling music. At last Joseph decided where to place the Grail. When it was done we gathered around the "hiding place."

The Sun had already started its journey westwards and begun to assume a reddish color that shimmered like a rose-colored light across the surroundings. We sang a hymn that in solemn tones rose against the evening sky. Perhaps I imagined it, but I thought I saw the rose-colored light of the sunset sending its rays straight to the "hiding place," making it vibrate in a glowing pink-colored light.

Joseph spoke in his mighty voice. His speech will be imprinted in my memory forever.

"We are standing on the threshold of a new era," he said. "The Grail will sleep for at least two thousand years. Its healing power creates a forcefield that will increase as time goes by. When this forcefield has reached its climax, the Grail will not be hidden any longer. A certain human being will find it. Then it will be time for the world to make amends for all the evil and be healed by the Grail's rays. The Masters of the Great White Brotherhood will materialize to confirm that the time has arrived. The Earth will be on the verge of a breakdown and the Grail is meant to be a link in its healing. At this time the Earth will be a battlefield for different religions which will have emerged from within Christianity as well as outside of it. Brother will kill brother, father will kill son. Humans' self-interpreted religions will spread violence, evil, and assault. Temples will be dishonored and demolished. Nothing will be sacred. It will be honorable to misinterpret, ruin, and destroy.

"Ancient wisdom tells us that there are, and always will be, ancient Truths, which are to be found as the basis of all religions and belief systems that emerge. People are different and live differently. That's why they adapt their beliefs to where they are living and give their gods different names, even if all these have their origin in the one and only God.

"The ancient wisdom also tells us that there is a cosmic world that contains the Wholeness which cannot be measured by science, but which is real. Every one of us has a spark of the Divine in us, and therefore we can all come in contact with God. The Divine is the foundation of all existence. Consciousness of this does not come from the church, but is something that gives peace, perfection, and Divine trust.

"Beauty and Love will always be there. Beneath everything, behind everything, a joyous song of Hope will be heard. It is the victory over evil – the victory of Beauty and Love. We all sing that song. It will become our battle song. And we will be many. Masters of the Great White Brotherhood will be reborn among people, in order to help humanity. The Earth will blossom and flourish again, just as it does here. The power of the Grail will be heard deep within the Earth. Let there be Light – and there is Light!"

We went down the hill in silence. Lydia and I were holding hands. We knew.

22. Back to Mary Magdalene in Massilia

Joseph of Arimathea told us he would return with us because he wanted to bring Mary Magdalene and her daughter to Egypt. There they would wait for Jesus. Both my part and Lydia's were finished until further notice. It was time for us to return to the Angelic Realm to get new missions. I felt a little disappointed not to be allowed to see more of the South of Gaul, but Lydia comforted me. There were to be more peep-holes.

"There is another version of Mary Magdalene's flight to France," Kualli told me when we had come back. "Joseph of Arimathea helped her to escape to Egypt directly after the Crucifixion. She had the baby in Egypt. When Sarah was twelve years old they went to France. The child is said to be 'black,' and was later on called 'The Black Madonna.' But the word black was the word for grief, not for skin-color. She was also called princess, since she was a descendant of the dynasty of David."

"Which version is the right one?" I muttered. "Do you know? There are several versions that do not mention Mary Magdalene as the spouse of Jesus; instead they say he was married to Mary of Bethany. They say that the Bethany sisters and their brother Lazarus also came from the dynasty of David. Then Lazarus must have been the royal heir? Martha was the oldest one, and what happened to her? Today some people in Provence say that she and Lazarus were on the boat that arrived with Mary Magdalene. That must be wrong. I never saw them on the ship, but I met the nice boy Maximin."

"Look, Jan, all this happened about two thousand years ago. Do you really think we would make these peep-holes of Truth for you if they led you to the wrong place?" Kualli smiled. "We are far from ready yet, but I understand that you must ask questions and sometimes also feel doubtful. How did you like Joseph of Arimathea?"

"He was okay," I answered happily. "He was a learned man with a keen intelligence and a broad perspective on life. A champion of the Truth and a wonderful support for Mary Magdalene."

"Can you imagine parallel worlds?" Kualli continued by asking. I lifted my eyebrows. I found the question irrelevant in this context.

"Of course, there are many parallel worlds that tell the same story in different versions," I answered. "Perhaps all I experienced in the peep-holes was only a fairy-tale in this world and reality in another? Where are you going with this?"

"People can dive unconsciously into parallel worlds when they look for the lost or the vanished," Kualli stated.

"Is that what I've done?" I asked, surprised.

"Not you!" Kualli laughed. "You are guided from here. Do you think we send you through these peep-holes at random because we think it's fun? But it's easy to get confused when you know or believe you know the same incident has many different courses of events. We must stick to one reality here and now. Here is the Angelic Realm, where you dwell right now. Your past is on Earth, which we have strong ties to. It is that Earth we work with, it is that Earth we make peep-holes into, and in them things can only turn out one way. That is what you are working with all the time now.

"We are going to send you back to the South of Gaul (current Provence) twelve years after your first visit. It's time for you to see Mary Magdalene again. We don't want you to go around wondering what happened next."

"So I am going to the cave where she lived for thirty years?"

"No, not at all. However, you are going back to the 'Roman house' where she lived with her daughter and her friends until she was on her own."

"Did she visit Jesus in Alexandria at any time?"

"You can ask her. I believe you will ask her many questions and she will surely answer you. But avoid talking about David."

These were the orders I was given before the next peep-hole, which I considered a very good name for my excursions into the past.

I was standing outside the white house. Since my last visit, a forest of multi-colored flowers and bushes had grown up, but the house itself looked the same as before. I knocked at the door and it was immediately opened by a young girl in a white dress. This must be Sarah, I thought. She had her mother's beautiful hair, but without the auburn tints. Her hair was deeply brown-black but her eyes reminded me of her father. They held many nuances of color and were big and long-lashed. Her face was very like Mary Magdalene's.

"Who are you?" she asked.

I made the Essene greeting in order to see how she reacted. "Peace be with you," I said. "I'm the Angel Jan. Your mother knows me."

"Peace be with you," she answered, smiling, and I saw the same deep dimples in her cheeks as Mary had. "I'll fetch her."

She had just turned around and then Mary stood there, as radiantly beautiful as always, but her eyes spoke of grief. When she saw me she hugged me warmly and took me into the house. At first we just sat down and looked at each other. Then both of us started to laugh and she took my hands.

"Where is Lydia?" was her first question.

Goodness, I had totally forgotten Lydia. I had not the slightest idea if she had accompanied me or not, but I didn't have time to finish that thought before she appeared from nowhere in her sea-green dress and embroidered shawl. Mary cried for joy and the ladies fell into each other's arms. Well, I thought, there shouldn't be any earthly feelings involved when two Angels visit the past. But there were. Feelings are easy to carry with you, bringing you sorrow and loss, but also, of course, love and joy.

When the initial female gossip was over with we sat on a comfortable divan and now I could start asking questions. Sarah came with a tray of small, sweet cookies and glasses with refreshing juice. She asked a little hesitantly if she might sit with us, and her mother nodded.

"Did the three men – Nicodemus, Joseph of Arimathea, and Benjamin – come back here properly from Britain?" was my first question. "And where are they now?"

"Yes, they came back here and rested after their long journey," answered Mary Magdalene. "Nicodemus has left for a missionary tour around Gaul, together with Benjamin. Maximin is still here. He doesn't want to leave me; he looks upon himself as my chosen protector. Joseph, the indefatigable, brought Sarah and me to Alexandria in Egypt to see my beloved husband. His name is no longer Jesus or Yeshua. For safety reasons he calls himself different names, since the Romans could have spies also in Egypt. Mostly he lives in Heliopolis, in the magnificent monastery located there. We met in Alexandria at the house of mutual friends. Sarah was only two years old. She cannot remember much of that meeting, but Jesus was overjoyed to see her."

"And you?" I asked, since I saw a shadow passing her pretty face.

"I miss him," she whispered, and the tears welled up in her eyes. "My whole life is built on the lack of the person I love the most and who I am a part of. We couldn't stay long in Alexandria. Yeshua lives as a monk in Heliopolis; it's his best protection for his remaining mission. He promised to come here if his heavenly Father tells him it is the best way. If not, we are going to visit him again. And that will happen very soon, I believe."

"What do you do here?" asked Lydia, putting her arm around her friend. "How do you pass the time?"

"Time passes swiftly." Mary smiled. "I have our daughter Sarah to bring up in the spirit of my husband. I convert people. You cannot imagine how many people I have already converted to the wisdom teaching of my husband. I also travel around with Maximin and Sarah and talk to people. You were lucky that we were at home now. We are resting after a quite troublesome journey in the North of Gaul."

"Have you heard anything more about the Grail?" I asked.

"No more than you," was the answer. "But I know that Joseph of Arimathea returned to Britain after he had been with us to Egypt and back. That man loves travelling. He is like a fish in the water when he is aboard the ships, and all the captains love him. He has laid the foundations of the first Christian church in Britain, in Glastonbury, where you were. As far as I know, he is still there. I hope he will come back and visit us when he is finished with Glastonbury. Maybe he is keeping a watchful eye over the Grail; I don't know."

"How do you work?" I asked.

"I prefer talking to people," she answered. "I stand in the marketplace and start talking. People crowd around me, and most of them are good at listening. I don't often get heckled or garbage thrown at my head. It has happened – but not often. But as you know I also help sick people. I have done that a lot here. It makes me happy, because it makes the people happy and makes it easier to convert them."

"Mary Magdalene, did you write a gospel?" I asked seriously. She stared at me for a long time.

"Where did you hear that?" Now it was her turn to ask a question. "The only thing I write is letters to my beloved, and sometimes I receive his letters by boat. I don't know anything about any gospel. Everything is in my head, in my mind. I preach words that I'm not really aware of; I get unconscious inspiration that leads me like a star. I believe it is my husband sending the inspiration to me."

"I have good news for both of you!" said Lydia. "That's why I was a little late. We – Jan and I – will go with Mary and Sarah to Alexandria – now! Jesus will meet us there. What do you say about that?"

Mary plunged up from the divan and embraced Lydia. Tears of joy were running down her cheeks. But Sarah sat pale and still, with discouraged eyes. She didn't show any feelings at all.

"Next week is Sarah's birthday," her mother announced. "She will be twelve years old. What a lovely birthday present, dear!"

After these words Sarah silently arose and left the room. Lydia stopped Mary, who wanted to follow her.

"The girl needs to be alone. She has not met her father for ten years; you must understand that she has mixed feelings."

"It's a long voyage at sea," I interjected, knowing I was talking for myself as well. "It might be strenuous. Maybe she worries about the trip. But, by the way, where is the Arab? Couldn't he comfort her? He seemed so fond of the child during our trip."

"He has left us," Mary answered. "When he heard that David was alive and lived in an Essene monastery at Lake Garda, he went there. I hope he was welcomed there. I sent a letter with him."

The girl was not worried about the trip; she was worried about seeing her father again. For her, he was a long-distant stranger she had learned to live without. She now asked her mother to be spared the voyage. Maximin could take care of her. But Mary didn't accept that. The result was that we brought a sulky little lass with us, who refused to talk to us and answer our questions. Mary was in despair, but Lydia told her the girl's temper would pass. Many thrilling things had happened when we at last came ashore after a long and weary trip, which was a bit shorter than the last one. The trip wasn't exactly enjoyable, at least not in my opinion. But I had succeeded in cheering up the girl by talking to her and telling her stories about her father and the country we were going to visit.

23. Mary Magdalene's Story about Her Early Years

We sat on deck and the evening was clear and calm. I noticed the difference between Mary Magdalene now and twelve years ago. She was more mature now, and above all, she had more authority. The soft, young, pregnant woman was no longer there. Instead she was an experienced woman, rich in both disappointments and joys. Wherever she went she got a lot of friends, and I could understand why. And now at last Sarah's sulkiness had disappeared with the waves and she was lying with her head in her mother's lap, chewing a date. Lydia was looking out to sea very dreamily, and I wondered what she was thinking. Maybe she was thinking about the same thing as I was?

I suddenly got an inspiration to ask, "Mary, nobody knows anything about your life in Magdala. You were at least seventeen years when you came to Jerusalem. Why did you go there? Who were your parents? You have never spoken about them. Would you please tell me?"

She looked at me with her big, beautiful eyes and blew away a persistent wisp of hair which shone a deep auburn in the soft light of the evening sun. "There's not much to tell." She smiled, but there was great grief in her eyes. "My parents are dead. But I will tell everything to the Angel Jan and my dear friend Lydia, both of you who stand so true at my side. Sarah has already heard it, but she can hear it again.

"I was born on a windy night in the prosperous market town of Magdala. My father, whose name was Jonathan, told me about my birth. My mother was very beautiful and very wise, and he loved her tremendously. I have only heard that she was a very good and generous lady. My parents longed to have a child, but I took my time. There were complications at my birth. Father called for all the healers and midwives he could find. Therefore, there was a rich collection of knowledgeable people around my birth. My father sat at Mother's bedhead, held her hands, and caressed her curls. But when at last, after a long and difficult delivery, I was born, my mother died.

"I presume my father had wished for a son, but he never told me. No child could have wished for a more tender father. I have really been loved. Even though my father was a brilliant businessman and had created a large fortune, he had time to give me much love. Apparently I resembled my mother, with her hair, her eyes, and her sweet manners. Certainly I was brought up to a great extent by servants, but each of them were chosen, true, and reliable.

"Father had a servant who was his jack of all trades. This was Saddhim, the Arab. Sometimes he was just called 'The Arab'; I don't know why. He became like a second father to me, perhaps more strict, but always just and clear in his judgments.

"Now I will tell you a little about my birthplace, the town of Magdala, where I grew up, as cherished and taken care of as a greenhouse-flower. Magdala is the Jewish name of the town and Tarichea the Greek name – but you know that, don't you? We had a big fishing fleet and even a theater. The name Magdala means 'fortress' and Tarichea comes from tarichaeon, which means 'drying fish.' I tell this in order for you to understand that the dried-fish trade was a great source of income that my father was quite involved in. My home town was near the western shore of the Lake of Galilea (see the map on page 35).

"When I came to Gaul I was overwhelmed by the vegetation. I found the same trees and flowers that belonged to my childhood: fig, walnut, olive, and palm trees, not to mention all the vineyards. My father in Magdala also traded in textiles, because he owned a dye-house. As I grew up I was inquisitive and eager to learn, and therefore my father made sure I got all the teaching he thought I needed. I was not his son, but I was almost regarded as a man by the surrounding people, since I learned so many things that otherwise were intended for boys exclusively. I am tremendously grateful for that.

"In fact, we also lived under the Roman yoke. In our town gathered people of all kinds, religions, and tribes. From childhood I saw people of different colors, heard so many languages, and learned about so many customs. Through this I got a kind of all-seeing that made it difficult for me to be judgmental. To me humans were … just humans! I got opportunities to wander around the town and visit markets, always accompanied by the Arab and a couple of women from the household. I was allowed to be present at horse-races, which I enjoyed.

"The best thing I knew was when my father was home and put me on his knee and told me about my mother. We would cry together when he described in detail how beautiful she was and how wisely she always acted. She was generous to poor people, and anyone who came into her vicinity loved her. I also wanted to become such a woman. My mother has been my ideal since I was a small child, and yet I never knew her.

"There were often disturbances and violence in Magdala. I believe that was the reason that one day when I was fifteen my father gave me a pretty little box in private. 'In that box you have the address of your uncle and aunt in Jerusalem,' he said. 'If something should happen to me, your uncle – my dear brother – will take care of my fortune until you're grown up or marry and need a dowry. He and his wife are prepared to take care of you if necessary. Primarily it will be the Arab that will help you if I come up against something. The next step must in that case be Jerusalem and my brother. Don't ever forget that, beloved daughter.'

"I had reason to remember this earlier than I expected. There were often riots at night in the town, but not near our house, which was situated in a genteel area; there were too many guards. But one night when I had just fallen asleep I was awakened by loud exclamations of horror. The Arab darted into my room and told me to instantly get dressed, pack some necessary things, and put on a dark cloak. Tears streamed from his eyes, and when I asked him about my father, he didn't answer, but told me to hurry up. He was waiting outside my room with two crying women.

"Behind the house was a beautiful garden. The exit of the garden was at the rear, and we snuck out that way. When I turned around I saw an alarming fire light.

"'Hurry up, Mary; tomorrow we have to go to Jerusalem,' the Arab whispered, and I could feel his big hand, holding mine, tremble. I felt in my pocket to see if the little box was still there. It was in good hands. All four of us hurried away on back ways to the lake. There we entered a cottage which belonged to one of the fishermen. Father had employed many fishermen, and I knew he was a popular employer. Sometimes I went with him to visit the families of the fishermen. We brought eggs, flour, and other necessities for them. This particular fisherman was one of his most capable. The man was at home, and he greeted me reverently. He exchanged a worried look with the Arab, who nodded to him.

"'You see, little Mary,' the fisherman said, but he didn't get any further. A sob stopped him.

"'Where is my dad? Has something happened to him?' I cried out, while my anxiety spread its icy coolness, slowly creeping up my legs and arms all the way up to my head. 'Where is he? Will he come here? Why is it burning over there?'

"The fisherman's wife placed me carefully on the long bench in front of the table. She sat close to me, ready to comfort me in the manner of women or mothers. I needed all the comfort I could get. My father was dead. I never knew that he was a member of the resistance against the Roman occupation. I didn't know he was the leader of a secret organization that wanted to get rid of the Romans and the violence from our town. I knew my beloved father – and yet I did not know him at all. I wept out my sorrow in unknown, soft arms, and unknown gentle hands dried my tears. One of the houses on our street had started to burn, and nobody knew who had started the fire. Flight was the best option. The Arab saved my life.

"The fisherman's wife made her children's bed for me, while the children slept on the floor. She made the bed with clean linens and with a lot of love.

"'You and your father visited us when we were badly off,' she whispered in my ear. 'There were times when we had no fish, and starvation was imminent. But we never starved, thanks to you. Now we have an opportunity to pay back a small amount of our debt. May all gods take care of you, dear child!'

"At last I fell asleep to a delightful melody sung by a lovely female voice. The fisherman's wife sang the lullabies she used to sing to her children when they were little. There was no help for me. Father was dead, and I would never see him again. But the warm, quiet voice gave me the comfort I needed in the most difficult moment of my life. I can still hear it in my inner ear.

"With resolute steps Saddhim, the Arab, lead a donkey, who recently had been purchased for an eventual trip. I sat on the donkey, holding its tousled mane in a tight grip. It even felt like the donkey belonged to the kind ones. From that moment I divided people I met into two categories: 'the kind ones' and 'the others.' Not 'the evil ones.' At that point, I hardly knew what evil was. Sometimes I still believe it doesn't exist. Grief I know well; it is my constant companion. But if you can marry grief with joy, you will get better thoughts and emotions.

"The two female servants stayed with the fishermen, since that's where they had come from. Now it was just the Arab and me. The little box was resting close to my bosom; it felt safer there. The Arab brought some simple food for the journey: bread, dried mutton, and water. There were not many hardships on our journey to Jerusalem. We met some occasional wanderers and horse-men, but none of them cared about a young girl and her Arabian companion. I was thinking a lot during that journey. What would happen to our beautiful house? Where did the other servants go? Where was the body of my father? Why did I not get the opportunity to say farewell to him?

"The Arab couldn't answer me. He looked at me with a tired and sad look and said he hoped my relatives would take good care of me. If they didn't, he would put them straight, he added, and I felt safe when I looked at his tall, muscular figure.

"I had met my uncle, his wife, and my three cousins when they visited us in Magdala. They had visited us many times, and I knew that my uncle Josephus and my father were very attached to each other.

I remembered them as sweet and kind people, not like 'the others.'

"We were received with the greatest delight. When uncle Josephus found out the reason for our 'visit,' his delight turned into dismay. The letter, which had been carefully folded together with my uncle's address, was posthumously with a prayer to my relatives that they would let me live with them and with instructions about where to find my fortune. My uncle knew how important the Arab had been to my father, so he was not shown to the servants' quarters. He got his own room and was told to rest after the long journey. Aunt Anna told me to do the same.

"Now a new life started. It took some time before my new family and I got to know each other. Their children, two girls and one boy, were already married.

"'Actually, you are of marriageable age,' my uncle said, with an mischievous look. 'I'm sure we will find you a good husband.'

"'Don't you frighten the girl,' my aunt protested. 'First of all she must get over her loss.'

"'Well, when it comes to money,' my uncle resumed, 'don't you worry, dear. Your father has deposited your inheritance here. The only thing you have lost, besides your father, is the house in Magdala.'

"It didn't appeal to me to marry some unknown man who perhaps I didn't want at all. I decided to find someone I could love. I knew I had very deep feelings, that I wanted to love and to be loved. I also had knowledge that no man should despise. I didn't want to be a man's housekeeper, which most women were. I wanted a man with whom I could talk. Soon I would find him."

"At the Baptism," I interrupted, "you sent him the dove."

"But many things happened before that," Mary Magdalene continued. "We had met a couple of times; I had been present when he spoke in Gethsemane and some other places. I had kept myself in the background. On one occasion we met at the house of Mary, Martha, and Lazarus. My Aunt Anna was acquainted with both the mother of Jesus, Mary, and the brothers and sisters in Bethany. We were invited by them, I found out later, because Josephus and Anna wanted to introduce a heathen girl. That girl was me. But one thing was for certain: I fell deeply in love with Jesus the first time I saw him. On that occasion he didn't see me. In Bethany I understood that Mary, Martha's younger sister, was also in love with him. I didn't hesitate for one moment about my feelings; that was the man for me: him and no one else. And that's what happened. Maybe I transferred some of my love for my recently deceased father to Jesus. But that was only in the beginning. I wanted to love, and eventually – well, quite soon – I was loved. The dove was just a holy joke. I knew he loved doves and I trained one for him."

"The fact that the dove was alive. Did he understand the message?" I interrupted again.

"For him it was a message of my love. He saw the dove and felt it sitting on his shoulder. In that moment I knew that it was him and no one else. Only him. The next time we met we both knew. It was in the Gethsemane garden, where important things were happening.

The faithful Arab had become part of my new family, and everybody loved him. He wasn't regarded as a usual servant, rather more like a friend who you could ask about everything. He was the one who came to me with a message from Jesus, who wanted to see me in the herb garden.

"His disciples were assembled around him. When I arrived there and stopped hesitantly outside the crowd of men, he saw me, and he asked them to wait. He came straight towards me and took my arm. We went to a secluded part of the garden and I felt the looks of the disciples on my back. Not all of them were friendly. Some of them belonged to 'the others.'

"That was when he proposed to me. That was the first time I felt his arms around me and his mouth on mine. That moment I felt that the world could collapse unless the two of us got to be together. There was only one word I could answer him: Yes! I don't think he told his disciples that we were going to marry. They might react negatively if the Master got married. Jesus went to my uncle and asked for my hand. It took some time before my uncle gave his permission. I was free, but a minor.

"When the day finally came when we were wed, it happened in utmost secrecy in the atrium of my relatives' home. Only my uncle, my aunt, the Arab, and the three brothers and sisters in Bethany were present. It hurt to see the suffering of Mary of Bethany. She said she didn't feel well and went home soon after the wedding ceremony, so she was not present at the supper."

"Did you and Mary from Bethany become enemies?" I asked carefully.

"No, but I don't know what she felt in her heart. I liked her; she was a nice girl. Afterwards I heard that she was present at the Crucifixion and that she came to the grave and found it empty. I also know that she met Jesus in the graveyard. He was there on a particular matter. She was not allowed to touch him, but that was because he still was so weak and so badly damaged after the Crucifixion that he had pain everywhere. He shouldn't have been there, but you know how stubborn he is. During the occasions when he thereafter appeared to people, it was actually him and not a spirit. He let the disciples believe that he appeared from another world, because he would otherwise surely be caught and crucified again. You know, some of those boys cannot keep a secret. In addition, they are jealous of me, so they are probably happy that I disappeared. Meanwhile, when all this was happening, I gave birth to his child. Life is strange, isn't it, Jan?"

"Yes," I agreed. "We have to hang in there. But I wonder, what happened to the little girl, Mary from Bethany?"

"She is married and still lives in Bethany," answered Lydia.

"Thank you for telling us your story, Mary; it was lovely."

I was thinking that walking into another person's thoughts and feelings is like diving into a tunnel where you know that both clean and contaminated water flows down the walls. I felt as if I had been in that tunnel and that it was mostly clean water flowing there. At last Mary Magdalene became more real to me, more vivid than before. It felt wonderful.

24. Jesus As a Monk in Heliopolis, Egypt

I am not going to tell you more about the boat trip, which only stopped twice: once in Sicily and once in Crete. The best memory from this trip is the story about Mary Magdalene told by herself. It made the greatest impression on me.

In the little inn in Alexandria we first arrived at, we met Jesus, dressed as a monk like me. He embraced us warmly, and I saw tears on his cheeks when he hugged his daughter. I believe she was moved, because she stretched on tiptoe and kissed him on his cheeks. I was happy to see her mother's joy.

Heliopolis had once been a magnificent, giant city (see the map on page 35). To view this masterpiece from the past with modern eyes felt really remarkable. At the time when Jesus lived there, there weren't many temples left, but the big Sun temple brooded like a gigantic golden birdcage in the middle of the city. We checked into an inn on the outskirts, from where we could see the outlines of the shiny gold temple, among an abundant vegetation. I thought it was sad to know that all this beauty would disappear and the rest of the lovely city would be buried beneath the suburbs of Cairo. So I fully enjoyed the beauty and the mysticism of the past. Even more, I enjoyed the meeting with the Master from Jerusalem. Both here and in Alexandria, he now walked safe from the hatred of the Romans.

But didn't he ask for more than that? The life of the Savior had become an escape and the lonely life of a monk. Was that really what he desired? I decided to ask him.

"Are you content with your life now?" I asked, as we sat around a table in an undisturbed corner of the inn. "You can never return to your role as Jesus, the Savior. How do you feel, living here in isolation?"

"I was waiting for that question," Jesus said, smiling, "and there are many answers to it. When I look at it from a family point of view, it really torments me. To not be able to see my beloved wife, or see our lovely daughter grow up day by day, creates a feeling of loss that becomes a big empty hole inside me. I have many very good friends, both here and in Alexandria, and we often meet and talk about what is closest to my heart: to preach the wisdom of my Father, to teach, and to heal. I write a lot, and I hope my scriptures will be kept far into the future. It is my only way to contribute to the future. I have a group that I teach in silence in Alexandria. The next generation, the one which Sarah belongs to, can perhaps spread the word without themselves suffering. Everything happens in silence, so silent that not even a bird, a dog, or a cat can hear it. Do you understand?"

We understood. We understood so well that we sat quietly for a long time. Sarah sneaked around, listening at the door and the windows, checking that no one was eavesdropping. The child was seized by the peculiar atmosphere. She crept up to Jesus and hugged him and kissed him on both cheeks. Then she went down on her knees next to him and put her head to his heart. She remained in that position for a long time, and I saw how moved our mighty Master was.

At last he took her face between his hands, kissed her mouth, and said, "You have royal blood. You must continue our line. If you can, please teach your father's words to the listless ones, the hesitant ones, and the bitter ones."

When Sarah returned to her chair at the table, her face radiated with a new insight. I wondered what had started to blossom in this girl's heart after her father's words and what was working in her creative imagination. I decided to change the subject.

"We have been to Glastonbury, hiding your Holy Grail," I said.

Jesus looked at me in a serious way. "Which one of them?" he asked, unexpectedly.

I gave a start. Was there more than one Grail …?

"The vessel, of course," I answered. "The lovely alabaster vessel. Your wedding present."

"That is certainly one of the sacred treasures," he said. He was smiling now. "The other one is sitting there!" He pointed at Mary Magdalene. I jumped high. His wife wasn't the Grail, she owned it, I thought. But Jesus leaned closer to me.

"The Grail is a symbol," he explained slowly, in order for me to understand. "It is a symbol for the male and the female in symbiosis. Haven't you understood that?"

"For me it is an object," I answered. "It behaved strangely as we were about to bury it in its hiding place. It was lit up with a fantastic light, as if it was saying farewell to the world."

"It probably was – for the time being," Jesus remarked with a smile. "But you must understand that the Grail also means something else. The unification of the male and the female into the Divine, into the Wholeness – does that tell you something?" I shook my head. He continued, "You are looking for the Truth. Here you have it in a nutshell, Jan. That's why the Grail has been so sought for, for thousands of years. It can reveal its own meaning to the one holding it. It gives insight, Jan, insight. That's exactly what I have been trying to do all my life: give insight. I don't want to create a new religion. I just want to tell the Truth."

"You have the Truth, and I'm looking for it," was my answer. "Most people know that we carry everything we want to know inside of us. But it is rather difficult getting in contact with your inner wisdom. That's why we prefer to search for it on the outside. Your Truth is not mine, and the other way around. Aren't there many Truths?"

"The greatest Truth is our proximity to the Father," Jesus answered. "Then we have the Word, the Tone, the Sound. The Truth can't take care of itself. It needs our co-operation. It has a tremendous power. If it doesn't, it is being used wrongly. You want to know what really happened in your world – I mean your former world on Earth. If you are reborn in another world in another universe, the Truth won't be the same. Then you won't remember this. Will you be looking for Truth there too?"

"Probably," I muttered. "But right now we are discussing the Earth

I was incarnated on and where I died and what happened there. I set up boundaries for my Truth. No splitting hairs, please! I am now in a peep-hole and it's thrilling. I suppose you are all Angels too, actually, aren't you?"

"Yes." Jesus smiled. "But in your century you have something called motion pictures. Imagine that the peep-hole is a film which you can enter. By looking at various events there, you can get an idea of the Truth that applied at that time. Do with that, Jan. We cannot go any further in the search for the Truth. But we can look around here, in order to give you an idea about how my world worked during the rest of my life in Egypt. After that, you can go to another century if you want, or visit my colleague Issa." He rose and beckoned us to follow him.

It was a walk I will never forget. Heliopolis was not only beautiful and interesting, it had an atmosphere that was stunningly mysterious and thrilling. Yet we only saw the outside, not the inside, except for the temple which was dedicated to the Sun god. Mary Magdalene walked in silence next to her husband and with tears in her eyes. His arm was around her waist. She leaned against him continually. The strong teacher and healer was suddenly just a weak woman, a loving spouse and mother. My heart was moved by seeing them. Sarah ran around wildly and asked a lot of questions. She was a breath of fresh air.

Lydia crept very near me and whispered, "Are you not happy to see the family together here?"

"I am. But why can't Mary Magdalene and the lass stay here?" I asked. "Why must they go back to France? Or why doesn't Jesus move to Gaul with her? He has lived here for a while now and he is familiar with Heliopolis; he ought to find new pastures."

"Now you are trying to change history again," Lydia laughed. "If he had gone with Mary, she would not have been sitting in a cave in her old age. But she did, didn't she? I think Jesus wants to stay in Egypt, where he is well protected from the Romans. There is still a price on his head, Jan. The damages from the Crucifixion have left deep wounds on his body – wounds that will not heal. It will take time. The girl must be married to a man of royal blood, so that the royal line may expand and remain in the future."

"Be married," I snorted. "Aren't the girl's feelings taken into account? It sounds cold and calculating; I didn't think that was the way of Jesus or Mary Magdalene. If Jesus has irreversible damage, I don't understand a thing. He healed and revived the dead – can he not make himself immortal?"

"He is already immortal, through his name and his work, Jan. I think it's time for you to leave this place!" Lydia smiled, and before I had a chance to think, she took my hand and we flew away. As usual, I didn't know anything until I woke up in the Angelic Realm.

"Welcome here!" said a well-known voice, and I looked into Melchizedek's friendly, smiling face. "We had to bring you home before you made too many changes. Mary Magdalene and Sarah are returning to Gaul after their visit to Egypt. Maybe we can visit them later on in Gaul to see what happened to the two lovely ladies. Right now we have other plans for you. If you seek the real Truth, you have to keep to the big events in the New Testament. So we'll keep to those."

"What happened to Issa?" I wondered. "The visit with him was so fragmented."

"You are going there now: a peep-hole in Kashmir, in the legendary Srinagar."

25. Revisiting Issa in Kashmir

The Sun shone straight into my eyes as I suddenly stood outside a house in Ishbar, at the lake Dal. It was not the same house as before; Issa must have moved, if this was the place he now lived. I knocked. The door was opened by a middle-aged woman with a kind and pretty face. She asked me who I was looking for and I answered, "Issa."

This proved to be Issa's daughter, and she showed me into the house, which was very spartanly furnished. Lydia wasn't visible, but I felt her presence.

Issa was now quite thin, and his hair was completely white. His long, white beard floated over a simple white cloak. When he saw me he stood up and embraced me warmly.

"It's been many years since an Angel visited me!" he exclaimed. "Here nothing is what it was. My beloved wife is dead and my children take turns helping me. I am called a saint. They can call me what they like; I work with those who need me, those who are seekers, and those who want to listen. I preach and I am a teacher. Why are you visiting me?"

"I wanted to know what has happened since my last visit," I answered. "Have there been many miracles?"

Issa laughed. He showed me into the garden and we sat down on a stone bench under a blossoming tree. It took time before he answered. At last he said, "You might say that! I will tell you about the miracle of Sandiman, who was crucified here because of his beliefs. He was a very humble man and my disciple. He was in jail for ten years for preaching the same thing as I do. I ought to have gone the same way, but strangely enough, I have escaped both prison and crucifixion.

"Many people were present when Sandiman was crucified. He didn't talk; he kept his head down and prayed. I was standing near him. I had done everything in my power to get him freed, and people around him loved him. I knew him very well, and I decided to revive him. At night, when he was taken down from the cross, many women were assembled around his body. I was also there, very close to him. I prayed and asked for his soul to come back to Earth, because his work here was not finished. On the third day Sandiman returned to life. He was wounded by the crucifixion, but he was as humble and loving as always.

"Naturally, the astonishment of the people was awakened. They had never experienced a dead corpse being revived after a crucifixion. The people offered him the throne of Kashmir. He did not want to be king, but they were so insistent, that at last he agreed. He became a dignified ruler."

"So you can revive the dead, as Jesus did in Jerusalem?" I asked.

"Not me, it is God's work," answered the prophet. "If He had not wanted it, Sandiman would have died on the cross."

"You should perhaps have been appointed to be king," I proposed. I admired the beautiful view. The house was near the lake where most of the people in Srinagar lived in their boathouses.

"This is my kingdom!" said Issa, indicating the view. "The boat-people need me and so do many others. I still wander around and talk to people. As long as I can, I will be a guide for the people here. They need comfort and spiritual encouragement. Poverty and illness are frequent and hard. I heal, I comfort, and I give."

"Where is Thomas?" I wondered. "I expected to find him at your side."

"Thomas has gone his own way the last twenty years. He has founded his own church in the South of India. His members call themselves 'the Thomas Christians.' He is still working near Madras, in Milapore. I will call on him when my time is nigh."

I looked at the erect spine, the clear blue-gray eyes, and the few wrinkles on his handsome face. "I hope it will be a long time before that happens," I said. "Maybe I will come here again."

"Would you like to share my simple meal?" he asked. My human body wanted to accept, but Lydia pinched me, so I declined. I realized that this was to be a swift visit and that we had to proceed into the motley world of the Bible. When we came outside the gate, I felt myself leaving the ground, and everything went black. The last thing I saw was Issa. He was standing at the door, waving his hand. He had a subtle smile on his face. He must have known where Angels come from!

"Why couldn't I stay longer with Issa?" I posed the question when I came back.

Lydia replied, "We have other important things to do. You won't be staying here for long, either."

I closed my eyes and thought about how I was treated. I would have liked to have stayed for a while in Srinagar and visit the people who lived in the houses on rafts on the lake. On the other hand, I knew that my peep-holes were not to be used for pleasure.

A laugh came from Lydia, who interestingly must have been following my thoughts. "Haven't you always wondered about the Immaculate Conception?" she asked.

"Oh yes, I have!" I exclaimed. "Jesus told me in Gethsemane that I would find out about his lineage later on. Is it time for that now?"

Lydia nodded in a secretive manner. "Maybe you think that we are doing this backwards," she resumed. "We have accompanied Jesus and Mary Magdalene at various times, yet we have not seen or heard anything of the Virgin Mary."

"I actually thought that Joseph was the real father of Jesus," I remarked. "I have always believed that the tale about her being pregnant when she married him was fabrication."

Lydia shook her head and took my hand. "Time for the next peep-hole," I thought, and closed my eyes.

"You are both right and not right," Lydia whispered to me the moment I woke up. We were standing outside a strange temple. At least I thought it was strange, or even better, impressive.

"The Essene Brotherhood is a part of The Great White Brotherhood, who has its residence both on Earth, in the Angelic Realm, and upwards,"

Lydia explained. "This is the Temple of Helios, situated in Jerusalem at one of the outer gates."

"Has Jesus been here?" I asked, gazing at the beautiful building.

"He is not born yet," objected Lydia, who was fully visible now and dressed in a long, white, glittering dress that suited her very well. "In a moment you will see what really happened and I will be your guide. I have created a kind of mist around us, because secret things are happening here. The Essenes have very secret ceremonies in this temple, where their highest officials, priests, and magicians meet."

I was shivering, although I was an Angel. This was unbearably thrilling!

"Mary's parents know about this organization," Lydia continued. "Mary has been summoned here now. She is only twelve, but soon she will be thirteen. Actually the law says no girl must marry before thirteen. Mary is a chosen one, even if she doesn't know it herself. However, her mother Anna and her father Joachim know quite a lot. Her father was a high priest in this temple. He knew that his wife would give birth to the girl who would carry the Messiah in her womb."

"Nothing is written about that in the Bible," I muttered. "But this thing about the Angel …"

"… is something you shouldn't worry about right now," Lydia filled in with a smile. "Calm down; we will be right there. You know where the One you call God exists, don't you?"

"In another universe, surrounded by seven smaller universes," I quickly answered. "Near the Central Race …"

"… is the Creator. He wants his creation, Earth, to receive a Divine Power, who dwells on its lovely body. He wants to send a Divine soul down to Earth …"

"I thought all humans had a Divine soul," I interrupted.

"You could say that, but this particular soul would operate with the Divine during his life here. At the same time, this Divine soul must have a human body, because the solely Divine would not have the same understanding of people's problems and their vulnerability as one who lives on Earth and shares their sorrows and troubles."

"I can understand that. But Joseph wasn't the father of Jesus, nor was an Angel, right? How did the whole thing happen? Was there some kind of Angelic substitute in the temple? Was Mary asleep or was she awake?" Lydia only looked secretive.

"Why did they choose Joseph to be her husband? He did not want to, did he?" I continued suspiciously. "He was a widower and he had several children, isn't that correct?"

"Yes, it is. But now it's time for us to enter," decided Lydia, and she took my hand. We went up the stairs and into the temple. We stopped at the door, because a magnificent, radiant splendor met our eyes. The hall we entered seemed to be of gold. All the decorations on pillars, benches, walls, and floors were mixed with gold, and when the sun shone through the open ceiling, the gold glittered in a way that hurt my eyes. No living person was there. In the background hung a drapery of rare beauty. Lydia whispered that it was woven by seven maids. The colors were green, scarlet, purple, and gold. The threads were of linen and silk.

We gently glided forward and looked behind the drapery. There was only a huge canopy bed, with pillars consisting of golden Angels, climbing towards the light. Above the bed there was a round window in the ceiling, with beautiful paintings. The window stood open to the night sky. Then we heard steps and swiftly returned to the hall.

26. The "Immaculate" Conception and the Birth of Jesus

A procession of seven priests in full canonicals marched into the hall. They lined up on either side of the drapery, with the priest who apparently was highest in rank among them in the middle. He was an earnest-looking man, with white hair and beard and a finely chiseled face with clear blue eyes. This was obviously Joachim, Mary's father.

Again the magnificently ornamented door was opened, and a man and a woman came in, dressed in long, white, shimmering cloaks. The man was impressive and very good-looking, probably about forty-five years old. He had brown, curly hair and beard and brown eyes. He instilled a sense of safeness and reliability. His features were regular and his forehead was high. He had a woman at his side – but you couldn't really call her a woman. She was a lovely child. She had very long, dark-brown hair and her face was exquisitely beautiful. Her big green-brown eyes with their dense lashes looked frightened. She compressed her lips as if she had a lump in her throat. I realized that this must be Joseph and Mary. When I saw her tender body, with its chest just starting to grow and her slim waist, I wondered how this child would be able to carry a child in her womb.

Joseph was holding Mary's hand. They went straight to the high priest and knelt in front of him. A long moment passed in prayer. The priest rose and put his hands first on the girl's head, then on the man's head. I waited for pigeons to come flying, but there were none of them. Instead, what I saw was a strange light around this odd couple. The priest signed for them to rise, and then he drew away the curtain. The same strange light was there, too, and lit up the room. I couldn't see any lamp anywhere. The light had a faint greenish hue.

Lydia pulled me in there. We stood in a corner, near the curtain. Joseph sat down on the bed and pulled the scared girl down next to him. I saw how frightened she was, even if she certainly had been prepared for this moment. Joseph tenderly kissed her lips and she didn't offer any resistance. She seemed almost passive.

"Oh dear! Imagine, I will be the witness of a holy coition!" I thought excitedly. I found it more jittery than smutty. Lydia's silent giggle told me she had "heard" my thought. But now the moment of seriousness had arrived. My whole immaterial body told me something would happen, and it did.

Mary lay full length on the bed. I couldn't see her face, because Joseph was on top of her. A firelight flared up; it was as if an enormous flame covered the entire bed. At first it resembled fire, then it turned into a sparklingly white light. I perceived, rather than saw, a spirit sliding down from the window in the ceiling – straight down from the night sky twinkling with stars. This spirit radiated a white, shimmering light so intense that even an Angel had to close his eyes.

At the same time I heard the sweetest music, and when I looked up to the ceiling I understood that I was experiencing Seraphim. Not even at the Angelic celebrations had the Seraphim participated. In an extremely tremulous moment, in a Divine, incomparable, wing-beating breath, the Word was whispered, spoken, sung, and mediated. This wondrous picture of two people merging together turned into a holy act.

Lydia sobbed calmly. A few moments ago I had felt exhilarated in an off-hand way; now I felt ashamed and full of reverence. There was no doubt that the seed of Joseph made Mary pregnant with a human child. There was also no doubt that this human child had Divine origin. I put my arm around Lydia and she leaned her head on my shoulder. The heavenly song slowly diminished and so did the light, until the pale-green light we had seen in the beginning was resting around the couple on the wide bed.

Joseph rose slowly and gave his hand to Mary. She looked like a sleepwalker, but she had a faint smile on her lips. Her pretty white dress was spattered with blood. She was no longer a virgin, little Virgin

Mary! Lydia and I hurried through the beautiful drapery. Eight people were waiting in the hall. The seven priests were still there and Mary's mother, Anna, had arrived, ready to take care of her daughter. Mary's parents conversed quietly with the priests. When Joseph and Mary came out from the drapery hand in hand, everyone who was present bowed deeply.

"You saw a wedding ceremony in the beginning, in front of the drapery," explained Lydia. "The high priest, Mary's father, united Mary and Joseph in a holy union. The Bible doesn't tell us any of this; it suggests she was more or less a harlot, in view of her surroundings. Don't you appreciate knowing the Truth, Jan?"

We had come out in the garden which surrounded the temple, and I sank down on a park bench. I was totally crushed. Lydia laughed her cooing laugh and sat down at my side. I believe we had become visible.

"Anna followed her daughter to the Helios temple," Lydia went on. "Joseph was together with them. His calm and loving behavior impressed everyone. After the 'marriage' they were invited to a love-feast with the priests, and tomorrow they will go to Galilee, to Joseph's home. Now you have gotten to know the Truth, Jan. It feels good to know that people will find out how it really was. It has taken two thousand years."

"But what about the royal line?" I wondered. "Who in their family was of royal origin?"

"Joseph was directly descended from David," Lydia answered. "Remember that David reigned from the beginning of the 1100s BC until about year 975 BC. Of course, the dynasty branched out, but it was still possible to trace the descendants who were pure heirs of the throne of Israel."

"But what about Mary Magdalene?" I asked. I wanted all the details. "It is said she was from the dynasty of Solomon."

"I don't know about that. But the dynasties after him were also branched out in different directions. It's a little unclear how the pedigree looks."

"The direct heirs were called princes and princesses. Was Joseph a prince?"

"There were certainly hundreds of princes and princesses, and none of them were called royal unless they sat on a throne. Joseph had chosen to be a carpenter. He was a very humble and unobtrusive man."

"Anyhow, he could make babies," I commented dryly. "Jesus had several brothers and sisters. Were they all royal?"

"No, only the eldest one in every family got that title, even though nobody could remember that far back. It was only when the people of Palestine received the news that Jesus was the Messiah, that the rulers in Israel were frightened. The word Messiah actually means 'the Anointed One.' In the Old Testament it says that the prophets continually admonished the people to look to the future, to the day when the Anointed One, the Messiah, would come and establish a perfect kingdom. It was the actions of these prophets which led to the accusations of Jesus. Without their prophecy he might have been able to keep on preaching and healing. There were several prophets at that time, but only Jesus was considered dangerous."

"Thanks for your help, Lydia. Can you tell me about the day when Joseph came home from work and found Mary pregnant and claimed he was not the father? Was it like that?"

"Come on," said Lydia, smiling, and I closed my eyes as I felt myself flying away from the lovely garden at the back of the temple. It fretted me slightly that she always had the upper hand, but she obviously knew a lot more than I about what should be included in the Bible but isn't.

This time we landed in front of a house in a lonely place, surrounded by trees and bushes. It was a standard house for that time, made with sun-dried bricks. A staircase on the outside led to the terrace on the roof. A donkey and its foal were peacefully grazing the grass outside, and further off there was a pen for goats. There was not only one dwelling-house, but several smaller houses nearby. One of them seemed to be a carpenter's workshop.

Behind the house was a well. Mary was standing there, trying to draw some water. Her belly was big now, and it suited her to have put on some weight. Her cheeks were red from strain and her hair was curled by moisture. At once I wanted to help her, but Lydia grabbed me.

"We are still invisible, Jan," she whispered. "You wanted to know what happened when Joseph came home from work, and it is about to happen! Mary is pregnant in her sixth or seventh month."

Suddenly we saw a man approach with swift steps. Of course it was Joseph. He didn't walk; he ran when he saw Mary. To my great surprise, she dropped the well string and ran towards him. She threw herself around his neck with such a force that he almost fell to the ground. We went closer, because I wanted to hear what they said to each other. He patted her lovingly on her stomach and put his head on it and listened. Then he kissed her and held her for a long time in his arms.

"I couldn't stand to live with cousin Elisabeth any longer," she said. "I longed for my home and I longed for you. And I wanted to tend to our animals myself."

"You shouldn't have come home before I returned," he reproached her. "You stayed with Elisabeth so that she could give you nursing if needed, and I have been worrying about you. The neighbor tends the animals when I am away, and I help him in return. It is nice that everything is fine, though. Now we won't separate, my love! I will stay with you."

It was as if Mary had grown with her task. Certainly she was very chubby now, but she had a more decisive expression around her mouth, and her smile was open and happy.

"Do you want to see the birth?" Lydia whispered to me. "Come on, let's go!"

"All good things come in threes," I thought, when I opened my eyes again. The conception, the home-coming from Elisabeth, and now the birth. It was nice to see things in a coherent manner. Would we be visible now? Lydia answered by shaking her head. "Maybe it's just as well," I thought, and looked around.

There are three different tales about where Jesus was born: in a crib in a stable, in a house, or in a cave. At last I hoped to find out which was the right one. For me, his birth had been in a simple crib that my father made of wood and straw. We children helped him make the figures in the crib out of clay and cones and whatever else we could find. Now I had to do with a completely different version, which was the Truth.

What my startled eyes saw was a cave. I understood that it was an Essene cave. The Essenes made their caves very large, and well protected from attack by robbers, who there were plenty of. Their caves were well-known lodgings all across Palestine. They were furnished like homes, with clean floors, decorated walls which were covered by mortar, oil lamps hanging from the walls, and air ducts for ventilation. From nearby wells, crocks with fresh water were always carried into the caves. This cave was, true enough, in Bethlehem. It was not at all a primitive hole in the rock that I saw. There was no water running from the walls, and the floor was not damp or uneven. Mary was lying on a bed in a room which Lydia explained was "the maternity-suite."

Again I was grateful that we were invisible, because it was pretty tightly crowded. Joseph sat on the bed, but the donkey wasn't to be seen. It was probably feeding outside, I thought. However, there was an elderly, rather fat woman on Mary's other side. Of course she was not mentioned in the Bible, I thought, because there were just members of the holy family.

When Lydia and I came into the room, labor had begun. I took the opportunity of leaving for a while, to look at the night sky outside. Night it was, and the stars twinkled as they should, but I couldn't see any moon. I could not decide which month it was, but the air was lukewarm and the grass green and succulent.

I remembered that the early traditions of the church stated that Jesus was born on the 20th of May, but some Fathers of the church said it was the 20th of April. There were even some priests who claimed that he was born at the end of January. The Fathers of the church at last decided the birth of Jesus to be at midnight between the 24th and 25th of December, because of the very ancient and mystical ceremonies that had become spiritual laws for them. Most Avatars (descending gods) were born about that time, and in Egypt the 25th of December was celebrated as the birthday of several gods. Osiris, Bacchus, and Adonis were also born on that date. It was simply a date rich in tradition. The ground didn't at all look like frosty winter soil. However, I saw a big, beautiful star in the sky. It moved slowly. For me it could have been the evening star. It had a faint rose color. I am not an astronomer, so I decline further star speculations. I went into the cave again. Then I heard a long drawn-out cry.

Jesus, Yeshua, had appeared. Breathily, Mary fell back on her pillow and the robust lady took the little boy in her hands and washed him carefully. It was the same procedure as always when a baby is born, but one thing was unusual. The beautiful pale-green light I had seen at the conception was there and calmly lit up the little cave room.

Joseph cried. He kissed the hand of his wife and she smiled. The midwife put the little newcomer gently at Mary's breast.

Lydia whispered, "This was how it happened. There are invisible Angels in here, like you and me. The air is full of love and gratitude. The supernatural is natural here and now, exactly as it should be."

"What about the three kings or Magi?" I whispered back.

"They are waiting outside," was the answer, and I hurried out of the room. I have always been curious about the Magi. Of course there were shepherds, because the plains outside the cave were covered with sheep. But who were actually the Magi? Were they three holy kings or were they something else?

When I was a child I found a golden thread on the grass. I tied it around one of the cones that represented the three holy kings. But the wise men of the East didn't need to be classy; I would rather prefer if they were not kings. Now I would know the Truth.

The men who stood outside the cave, waiting for the signal to enter, did not at all look like kings arrayed in gold and jewels. There were not three men, but seven, and they were dressed in gray-brown habits like monks. But their faces could not be mistaken; they were noble and wise men with unusual gifts. I could tell it by their behavior. Three of them entered the cave when Joseph came and waved them in. Their radiation was unusual and very loving. They were all carrying gifts, but I couldn't see what. I assumed it was the gifts which were described in the Bible: gold, frankincense, and myrrh. But I also think they brought more important things to the newborn: greetings from the Great White Brotherhood, with information about how the child should be taken care of and be raised during his early years. At least that's what Lydia stated.

More guests had hastened from Bethlehem. Mary's cousin Elizabeth and her husband, the priest Zachariah, came with their newborn son, John (the Baptist). He was six months older than Jesus. Both children had a huge task ahead of them.

It was time to leave the happy couple with the newborn boy. Lydia took my hand, I closed my eyes, and everything vanished.

27. The Cousins:
Jesus and John the Baptist

"I like it most when we materialize and can meet people more closely," I explained to Kualli when we had come back. "Now I feel like a mere spectator, but at the same time it was tremendously interesting to behold the Truth."

"There are certain events we cannot let you take part in," Kualli said, smiling. "Not long after Jesus was born, both couples had a difficult time. Joseph and Mary escaped to Egypt, where they lived with their friends Elihu and Salome in a place which at that time was called Zoan. Herod was worried about his throne, and he had ordered his soldiers to kill all the babies in Jerusalem. Elizabeth escaped up into the mountains with John, where she hid in an Essene cave. When Herod interrogated Zachariah as to where his son was to be found, he did not get an answer. Then Herod commanded one of his soldiers to murder Zachariah when the priest was deep in prayer in the temple. You must know about this already, Jan, so what do you think comes next?"

"Jesus himself told me about his life," I said. "But I haven't seen the important details, those that the intelligentsia disagree on."

"You have experienced the beginning of Jesus' life," said Kualli. "Do you want to continue with the heresies of the New Testament or return to your life here as an Angel?"

"I'd like to continue, please," was my swift answer, "and preferably together with Lydia, because she is a such a good and learned companion."

"Of course she is. She was once an associate professor in history of religion, and it's as important for her as for you to elucidate what really happened."

"I just wonder about one thing," I said pensively. "You told me that

Elizabeth and John hid in a cave when Herod's soldiers were looking for the boy. What happened after that? Mary and Joseph were in Egypt with Jesus. Who helped Elizabeth when her husband was murdered? John the Baptist is said to be an incarnation of the prophet Elijah. That makes him quite an important person, too, doesn't it?"

"Elizabeth lived with the Essenes up in the mountains. Joseph found out, and he arranged for Elisabeth and John to be brought to Zoan. Joseph and the cousins Mary and Elizabeth stayed there for three whole years with their children. They were taught by the wise couple Elihu and Salome. This was a kind of preparation for the missions of both children and it also helped Mary, Joseph, and Elizabeth to understand the deeper meaning of their children's tasks."

"At the beginning of the twentieth century there was a man called Levi," I interrupted. "He related many details about Jesus and John, about their childhood and their adolescence, but nobody believed him. Quite a few laughed at him, but there were persons who took him seriously. He wrote a book called *The Aquarian Gospel of Jesus the Christ*. I read it when I lived on Earth and I was rather shocked. Is he reliable?"

"Most of what he has written is true," answered Kualli. "Not many living people have had access to the Akashic Records – but he did. It was also the intention that he should shock. It was intended that people should be moved. You are diving into the Akashic Records now, Jan, because that's where your peep-holes are. You must know that Joseph, the women, and the children did not go back through Jerusalem. They didn't feel safe; the Romans had spies everywhere. They passed the Dead Sea and went through Engedi on their way home to Galilee. Do you want to know anything else?"

"Thank you. I've got to know what happened to them during the first three years after not having known anything about John the Baptist. Can you tell me in a few words what happened to the children prior to the age of twelve, before we continue to the next peep-hole?"

"Elizabeth stayed in Engedi with a relative, Joshua, who took care of her and the boy. There was a hermit called Matheno. He was an Egyptian priest who came from Sakkara. When John was seven years old, Matheno took him into the wilderness. They lived in a cave and Matheno educated him. When John was twelve years old his mother died, and Matheno was the one who took care of him. He sent John to the Essene school at Qumran, where he stayed for a short time. Perhaps it was mostly to give the boys, Jesus and John, a short time together before the seriousness began.

"Matheno then fetched John and they went to Egypt, to the temple of Sakkara, where Matheno was a Master. John learned the purification ceremony of Baptism and how to purify people by baptizing them. John stayed for eighteen years in the temple in Sakkara, until it was time for him to go out among the people as a precursor to the coming Messiah. During his time in the temple, John showed proof of perseverance and patience. He believed that he was God's warrior and he saw himself as sent into the field to prepare the way for his cousin. He used no physical weapons, but preferred symbolic ones. The latter perhaps contributed to his hot-blooded attacks on what he considered to be unfair.

"In the meantime, Jesus was taught by his mother, Mary. She taught him all the wisdom she had learned from her friends in Egypt. At Jesus' seventh birthday, his grandfather, the priest Joachim, asked him what he wanted for his birthday. Jesus answered that there were so many poor children who had no food to eat. He wondered if he was allowed to invite them to a birthday party. He was for sure, and he ran out to fetch as many poor children he could find. He came home with 160 children, all of them dirty and in rags. But they were given food, all of them, and Jesus was happy.

"When Jesus was ten years old, the family went to Jerusalem for the great feast of the Jews. When Jesus saw how they slaughtered innocent animals and called them sacrifices in the name of God, he was devastated. The highest priest in the Great Council was called Hillel. Jesus went to him and complained about the sacrificing of animals and said that God is a God of Love. Could Hillel perhaps help him to find this God of Love? The old priest was very moved, and he asked Jesus' parents if he could teach Jesus for a year. Jesus stayed in the Temple in Jerusalem and returned home when he was eleven. Joseph taught him carpentry and Jesus was a patient, but not very interested, pupil.

"Now Jan, shall we begin the next peep-hole in the Temple, when Jesus was twelve years old? It might be interesting to know what really happened."

"Okay, here we go!" I said merrily, and we went at once, Lydia and I.

"Don't think that the baby you saw recently walked around on his chubby legs and talked faultlessly," said Lydia when we opened our eyes. "He was brought up just like other kids. Mary nursed him as mothers usually do, and Joseph was a good father. The first years, Maria and Elisabeth received highly esoteric training by Salome and Elihu, which they could mediate to their sons later on. The only difference was that the latter made regular visits to the Essene Temple in Jerusalem, but that's not the Temple you see here. In this Temple is the Jewish priesthood."

I remembered that Jewish law said that all boys who were twelve years old must go through a ceremony at Easter in Jerusalem. This resulted in a migration to Jerusalem every Easter, and this time Lydia and I joined in. Moreover, we were visible now. We were pushed and shoved in a big crowd when we tried to get nearer to the holy family. Lydia, as usual, went first, and more or less dragged me after her. I was dressed in my usual habit while Lydia had a pleated, natural-colored dress and a golden ribbon in her hair.

The Temple was on a quite high mountain. We were already in the Temple courtyard, but all the pilgrims who were there had been forced to climb the mountain. Some were supported by friends and relatives, others were carried in palanquins, and there were also people who tottered and staggered, rather than walked. Many people had a long walk behind them.

Certain parts of the Temple were intended for "the heathens." That's where Jesus and his family went. The heathens only needed to attend the first two feast days. On the third day, ceremonies were held for the strictly orthodox. The fourth day was only "half-holy," and those who wanted to could return home. That was the day Jesus was to have his tests and be examined together with other children. This must be that day, because Lydia and I were here. We followed as close behind Jesus and his family as was possible, because we wanted to be present at his examination. We could pass for another couple of parents. Formally this was a registration that would give the Jewish church a complete list of the boys who would soon be thirteen and their religious beliefs.

Of course, we were not allowed to be present at the examination. In order to attend, we made ourselves invisible. The first questions which were asked were about the religious ideas of each boy – which of course could be derived mostly from their parents. All of the boys got specific questions, and most of them had learned in advance what to answer. Jesus gave much clearer and more detailed answers than the others. I will not repeat the questions; I believe they are the same ones that the priests ask today. The learned men who were asking the questions were surprised by the answers from Jesus, which differed significantly from his comrades' answers. I looked at the boy because I thought he would look cocky, but actually he didn't. Instead, he tried to explain his answers, and he did that both with humility and courage. The old men looked at each other with great surprise and asked him to stay when the other boys left the room. He showed a higher insight and a deeper theological knowledge than the other children. He was asked to stay until the next day, because they wanted a Council of the highest officials, priests, and teachers to examine him. Jesus willingly accepted.

"I will go and tell his parents that he must stay here," I whispered to Lydia, who, terrified, grabbed my arm.

"Now you want to interfere with history again, Jan!" she whispered angrily. "Just be quiet. Instead, you and I could take a walk and see if we can find a nice inn."

I was thinking about the high mountain which Joseph and Mary would have to climb up and down again, but Lydia didn't care in the slightest. We couldn't find an inn. At last we sat down under a big walnut tree outside the Temple and from there we returned to the Angelic Realm. Lydia thought we should sleep there, since it was a long time to wait until the next day. I can't deny that it was nice to tumble down in my own bed, even if it was just for a few hours. The next day it looked very solemn when we stood invisible in the big hall, where the High Council was assembled to have a look at the learned, young heathen. Jesus looked so young and vulnerable, standing in his white, almost ankle-length shirt. The Council had put together really complicated questions and they also asked the boy what plans he had for the near future.

Without faltering in his speech, Jesus told them that he was a special adept at the Essenes in Carmel and that he had been a pupil in their school since he was six years old. Furthermore, he told them that he intended to follow the wishes of the Essene Brotherhood and visit schools and universities in foreign countries, including the Mystery School at Heliopolis in Egypt. His most immediate plan was to visit the University at Qumran. He also said he wouldn't return to Palestine for many years. This made him unable to visit synagogues or become an orthodox Jew.

We never heard him say, "Don't you know that I should be where my Father dwells?" This line is a later invention, I'm pretty sure. The priests kept the boy only for examination and it wouldn't have been logical for Jesus to have said this.

"Do you want to see more?" asked Lydia. "His parents will be coming soon. Mary was worried about her son, so they only walked a short distance before returning to look for him."

"I've seen enough," I said. "Now I know the Truth here too. The Bible doesn't like the Essenes, and the Holy Book never admits that Jesus and his family belonged to them. I heard the boy talking quite fearlessly about his studies at Carmel and his visit to the Essenes at Qumran and also that he was not going to visit the synagogues any more. The priests had a problem there. They couldn't refute his words, because they didn't know very much about the Essenes. Where are we going now?"

"You have heard Jesus talk about the initiations in Heliopolis. He also told you about his journeys, and you need not hear more about them," Lydia answered. "I think we should have a look at what he did on his return home."

"He soon married Mary Magdalene," I said happily. "That's the most important thing."

"Well, perhaps we should look closer at what is written in the Bible," Lydia proposed. "There are completely different things written."

"He has told me a lot himself," I objected. "But we don't know much about Mary from Bethany and her sister and brother. It is obviously sensitive stuff. Likewise, I don't know that much about Jesus' relationship with the disciples and their journeys."

"Then we will have to remain invisible," Lydia decided. "Let's go to Bethany!"

28. A Meeting in Bethany

We saw a small house on a hill, situated in very beautiful surroundings, with many trees and flowers. We caught a glimpse of several houses in the background. Outside the house there was frantic activity. When we came nearer, we saw a plump woman baking bread outside the house and at the same time screaming orders to the rest of the family members. I realized that this was Martha, the domestic and efficient elder sister. Her homely face was red with excitement from working the dough, while the hens were running around her legs and a couple of bony dogs were sniffing at the ground. Mary, the youngest sister, ran in and out of the house. She was small, black-haired, and brown-eyed, with a rather big nose, but I thought that she was a pretty girl. She didn't appreciate her big sister's orders, but she rather stood and talked to her brother, who was digging near the house.

"Is this the place Jesus visits so often?" I asked, astonished.

"Not so often nowadays, after his marriage with Mary from Magdala. Obviously, it's difficult for young Mary; she worships the ground on which he walks. I don't think you will witness any jealousy drama, because they had too much respect for Jesus to do that. In addition to this, they didn't want to hurt him. Look, there he is, with his wife, Mary from Magdala. This is the time when they've just gotten married, and he preaches his faith in the region around Jerusalem."

"Are we visible?" I breathed in Lydia's ear. She shook her head and signaled to me to look and listen.

"How long are you staying?" exclaimed Lazarus and hugged them both. "I hope you will have dinner with us?"

"Yes, please, we can stay a couple of hours," Jesus replied. "I am going to the market afterwards to talk to the people there. I am planning a wandering, together with my disciples."

I saw two women looking at Jesus with Love. Both of them loved the man in him and also the Master. Only one of them had his personal love and gave birth to his children. But perhaps Mary Magdalene was not as enviable as the other Mary thought. Magdalene was to experience some hard times and an involuntary divorce from her husband. Mary from Bethany stood at his side to his last breath on the cross – or what appeared to be his last breath.

Lazarus was a very thin young man, almost lanky, with tousled black curls and laughing brown eyes. He also looked at Jesus in a worshipful manner.

I pondered for a long time about what made people worship this Master. I simply found that you couldn't avoid loving him. His eyes and his smile ignited a spark in everyone who saw him – a spark of Love. I was also pleased that he had Magdalene and that his feelings could be earthly. When I came to know Mary Magdalene better, I realized that they were also a perfect match intellectually. He was the Master and the Savior, but she was indeed a woman far beyond the ordinary.

I realized that we were visiting this family after Lazarus had been revived from the dead. I got even more convinced when Lazarus asked, "If I die again, Master, will you revive me again?"

I heard Lydia's familiar titter, but Jesus answered very seriously, "You never died, Lazarus. You were in a death-like coma. If you really had been dead, I would not have been able to awaken you. If my Father wishes a human to cross the boundary, it is not up to me to counteract Him. He has cosmic reasons which are out of my sphere. I do not go against my Father's will, Lazarus."

"Can you tell me, Master, what death really is?" asked Mary from Bethany, and I saw Jesus and his wife exchange glances.

"Death is the transition to a new life," answered Jesus. "Death is a kind of rebirth, and nothing to be afraid of at all."

"Then I want to die in a grove full of blossoming roses of all colors," said the romantic Mary.

Her sister Martha slapped her arm. "You are not going to die; you are going to help me with the food in the kitchen," she snorted.

Mary Magdalene rose and went into the house with the sisters. She looked over her shoulder at Jesus. Her eyes were full of both love and compassion for the little dreamer, who didn't like doing chores.

We peeped into the house where Martha was going to make a stew from lamb and vegetables. Magdalene helped her, but little Mary sat in a corner and sulked. "I don't need to help; there are two cooks already," she snorted. "And besides, Martha, you will be rid of me very soon. I have decided to follow the Master on his wandering."

Martha dropped a knife, which fell on her naked foot and left a long scratch. "Look what you made me do!" she screamed angrily. "Do you really think the Master takes small lasses with him? No, you will stay here, lassie."

"I can look after her," Magdalene assured her. "She can go with us if she likes."

In that moment I admired Magdalene. But Lydia dragged me out of the house. At the courtyard outside, where previously only Jesus and Lazarus had sat talking, there was now a crowd. We saw they were mostly sick people. They must have seen Jesus arrive and then hurried to the house. There were blind, lame, and various kinds of crippled people. One man was lying on a homemade stretcher. He looked as if he was dead.

Jesus looked at him. "Take him away," he asked the stretcher-bearers. "I can do nothing. My Heavenly Father has called him." Thereafter he turned calmly to the other patients, one at a time, even if they were crying, begging, singing, or misbehaving.

"I think we will go somewhere else," whispered Lydia. "You have seen the brother and the sisters in Bethany and their house. You can imagine what happens there, and it won't get any more fun than that. I can tell you that Mary of Bethany never gave up on Jesus. She loved him until she thought he was dead. When she got the news much later that he was alive and in Egypt, things happened! That's another Truth."

"Was she the one who anointed him with lovely scents and dried him with her hair?" I asked.

"No, that was Mary Magdalene," Lydia answered, irritated. "I'd better show you that Truth too, because people talk a lot about it. Come on!"

Again Lydia's small, thin hand led me through veils of time-mist. This time we didn't go that much forward in time. When the mists dispersed, we were standing in a quite big room. We were still invisible. There were the closest disciples and Jesus himself. I recognized the big room in Bethany, because it was the room we had just left. Martha was busy with food in one corner. The others were sitting on the floor, eating and drinking.

Suddenly the door opened and Mary Magdalene came in. The woman was a radiant apparition! So upright, so stately! Her long, mahogany-colored hair was brushed out, as was the custom for mourning women. She carried a bottle in her hands. Lydia whispered that its content was nardus oil from India. It was an extremely expensive oil that had existed for thousands of years and that was used on special occasions.

The room became completely silent. Everybody looked at Mary Magdalene. Now I saw Mary from Bethany sitting in a corner, her eyes full of tears. Martha was standing stiffly, carrying a dish of fruit.

Magdalene went to her husband and looked at him with her eyes full of pain and love. She started to anoint his hair, massaging the oil in with one hand. Then she rubbed oil onto his hands. The strong, acrid, but at the same time appealing scent spread through the room. When she poured oil on his feet, the bottle fell out of her grip and oil flowed in thick drops, trickling over his toes. She took a little cloth that she wore in the folds of her dress and started to dry his feet. She didn't use her hair, as it says in the Bible, but it fell around her face and covered her. She must have gotten oil in her own hair when she pushed away the thick coils. In the next moment, a ray from the setting Sun fell through the door, straight onto her head. It was like a flame of fire in her dark-red hair, a fire of love and sorrow.

This lovely scene was interrupted by an angry Judas, the son of Jacob. He ran forward and took the empty bottle of oil in his hands.

"What do you mean by this?" he roared. "Why didn't you give the poor the money that this expensive bottle of oil cost? Mary Magdalene is squandering money, while our beloved Master is suffering from the false accusations of the Romans." Some of the other disciples agreed. Simon Peter was especially vociferous.

But Jesus pounded his fists on the floor and said, "Mary Magdalene did the right thing. She gave me the extreme unction before what's going to happen to me. One of you will betray me, and it will certainly not be her. She has not used your money, and you very well know the significance of nardus oil. It can give me some soothing in my troubles."

He leaned forward and kissed Mary Magdalene, and the disciples didn't dare make any more objections. The other Mary sat with her face in her hands until her sister forced her to stand up. She stood with her back to the others in the room and I knew she was suffering. Again I slipped into the merciful veil of unconscious transport.

29. The Story of John the Baptist

"I want to know more about John the Baptist!" I exclaimed when I woke up. "Why do we know so little about him? Why is so little written about him? What did he do? How did he work? Did he approve of the marriage of his cousin? He is said to preach about purity, chastity, and purity again. You shouldn't drink wine, you shouldn't have sex – he came with a lot of embargoes. He could not have had so many emotional experiences when he preached like that. He seems to have been an angry man. What did Jesus think of him?"

"There were many things to arouse one's anger," said Kualli, appearing from nowhere. "Just as there are today, for example. There was so much evil, no tolerance for humans or animals. You want to get to know John the Baptist. We will make a peep-hole into his life, Jan. Some things you will experience yourself and other things Lydia can tell you."

Before I had the opportunity to ask more questions, we were on our way in the usual manner. We were standing in the desert. I have always thought that deserts instill hopelessness and endlessness. This one was probably no different, but here there were mountains with lots of caves. We stood in front of one of the caves. Now we were materialized to my great delight.

"This cave is called David's cave, but I don't know why," said Lydia.

A tall figure crouched in the entrance. He came out and he looked like a real caveman. I couldn't believe that this was the famous John the Baptist. He probably shaved before he went out preaching, I thought. His hair was wild and overgrown, but I suspected that underneath he might be a handsome man. Furthermore, he was dressed in hides sewn together. I could understand why the locals called him the wild man. I estimated his age to be about thirty.

Two sharp eyes looked at us, and an equally sharp voice asked, "What do you want? Who sent you here?"

Lydia answered for me. She said with her loveliest smile and her mildest voice, "We come from the Angelic Realm. This is Jan, and I am Lydia. We are sent from the future to find out how you work. When are you going out among the people to preach?"

He stared at us as if he didn't believe one word. Lydia made her usual bold stroke. She disappeared and then re-appeared on the same spot. "Do you believe me now?" she asked. He gave no answer.

Then it was my turn. "I seek the Truth. I thought you could give it to me. There are so many lies and erroneous stories in and around the Bible and the New Testament. I want to change this, but I need someone to help me. Can you do that?"

He muttered something I didn't hear, but showed us with a gesture into the cave. I was startled when I looked around. We were standing in a comfortable home. I was even more startled when he asked us to sit down on soft hides around a low table, not to mention how startled I was when a pretty young woman came forward from the interior of the cave. She brought fresh bread, honey, fruit, and dried mutton, with goat's milk to drink.

"Are … are you married?" I stammered. I remembered very well all the angry words he said in the Bible about marriage, sex, and love between man and woman. Another Bible Bluff!

"I have a woman, Siwannah, and I have three children: two daughters and one son. Is that what you came here for? Well, here you can see with your own eyes one of the many lies in your Bible. When I work, I live in the world my Father in Heaven has ordered me to enlighten, and when I want to be with my family, I live here. It's the same thing with my cousin and best friend, Jesus. Why is that so secret?"

"Your reality does not conform with your teachings," I answered. "You talk about chastity and condemn lust and desire, don't you?"

"We are talking about another kind of chastity, one that means something different to what you are implying," he answered. I saw a

184

hint of a smile on his lips. "It has nothing to do with your body; it's the chastity of the soul. That's the important thing. It's a question of your thoughts being pure and loving. What's wrong with that?"

"Nothing." I was eager to answer him. "You are preparing the way for Jesus, aren't you?"

"Yes," he nodded, "by the Baptism which will take place soon. The Baptism is the purifying process. Human beings cannot live without water. When I see all the impenitent ones, who only come out of curiosity, I feel furious, and angry words just pour out of my mouth. I can imagine that those very words are the ones recorded as a memory of the wrath prophet."

"Were you Elijah 800 years ago?" I asked him.

"Yes! How did you know?"

"Angels know more than humans," was my cunning answer. He had nothing to say to that. For the first time, he smiled broadly at me. I felt myself liking him. Here was someone who did not talk too much, but who carried a great burden of humanity and compassion.

"I like being a prophet," he told me. "It's the best way of getting rid of all the problems in this country. The people understand me and the rich are afraid of me. Soon I will talk to Herod. I could teach him a thing or two."

"Please don't!" I exclaimed. "You could actually be beheaded!"

"That's a risk I have to take. I am also working for the Truth. If those in power never get to know the Truth, there will never be any order."

With a gesture, he invited us to taste all the good food laid on the table. "Elijah worked at Gilgal," he continued, "and I pass on his work in the same place. His wrath is mine, but his love is also mine."

I was impressed by this remarkable prophet. The food tasted wonderful, and the beautiful Siwannah served us and at the same time gave John loving glances and smiles. It was strange to sit at the angry prophet's table and hear noisy laughter and screaming from his children outside the cave. As we were leaving, he, to my great surprise, took first me and then Lydia in his arms and hugged us warmly.

"I enjoyed the visit from the Angels," he said, and genuine Love shone from his eyes. "It feels like a good beginning to the way I have chosen. Tomorrow I will baptize the King and Savior."

"You were so quiet," I reproached Lydia, when we were out in the sun. "Why so tongue-tied?"

"I didn't want to disturb the little boys at their games," was the cryptic answer given during the trip to the next peep-hole.

I was pondering about the beheading of John. I wanted to know the Truth about that too. Lydia and I were sitting together in the Angelic Realm when I posed the question. It was really a shame that a young and handsome man like John had such a short life. He had so much to give to the world.

"It was an intrigue," Lydia answered. "John was the victim of people's pure, undisguised evil. At first he was thrown into jail because he had the effrontery to dare criticize Herod. He was tried several times and taken before the king and the queen. In fact Queen Herodias, the wife of Herod Antipas, had fallen in love with John the Baptist. Herod himself was madly in love with his young, beautiful stepdaughter Salome.

"Herod had a plan: If John was reprieved he could become Herodias' lover, and Herod himself could win his passion, his stepdaughter. John was called to the palace and the queen received him in private. She begged him to be her lover and he would have his freedom. John refused her persistently, and it was then that Herodias instead started to hate him. Meanwhile, the king promised Salome that she could express one wish and it would immediately be granted. When Herodias was informed about this she told her daughter to wish for John's head on a plate. When it was fulfilled and the servants showed this terrible deed to Salome, she was stiff with fright, but her mother was triumphant.

"John was buried near the graves of his parents. But what nobody knows is that John actually loved a woman he could never have. It was a passion without limits. She was married to one of his best friends ..."

"Mary Magdalene," I sighed, but Lydia shook her head.

"No," she answered. "That was what I suspected, too, but it wasn't."

I never found out who it was.

30. Mary from Bethany Visits Jesus in Heliopolis

"So much has happened outside history and inside people," Lydia said thoughtfully, without answering my question. "Not even Jesus was free from human feelings like jealousy and suchlike. He sent his Magdalene to Gaul. It was his intention to preach his wisdom for the rest of his life, but something unexpected happened. I don't think you want to make a peep-hole there; instead I prefer to tell you about it.

"Mary from Bethany married a year after the Crucifixion. Her sister and brother wanted her to be a housewife in her own home. There was a widower who had courted Mary for a long time in a unobtrusive way. He had no children. Mary used to tease him, and sometimes she could be really mean. He forgave her everything and he was very insistent that she would marry him. He had been in the circle of disciples around Jesus, so he had the same beliefs as the brothers and sisters in Bethany. His name was Samuel.

"At last Mary said yes and they were married, not because she loved Samuel, but because she was tired of his nagging and her brother and sister's. It couldn't be worse to live with Samuel than with her exacting sister Martha. The marriage was not happy.

"Mary was a bad housewife. Mostly she sat dreaming. She did not become pregnant. The kind Samuel got tired of her talk about Jesus, how wonderful he was, and how much she had learned from him. After a few years they divorced. After the divorce, Mary found out that Jesus was alive and that Mary Magdalene had escaped to a foreign country. Now was her big chance – at least that was what she thought.

"Without telling anybody where she was going, Mary went to Alexandria. From there it was not far to Heliopolis. There was a problem:

no woman was welcome in the monastery. Mary procured a monk's habit, tied up her hair, and covered her face with soot. Now she looked like a young monk who had had a rough time on the road. She called herself Marius and she avoided talking more than necessary. After her arrival in Heliopolis she found out that Jesus, the hierophants, and the other Masters visited the main Temple at certain times of the day.

"When Mary saw Jesus again her heart started to beat violently, her knees gave way, and she wanted to shout out her love and longing. When she fell on her knees, one of the young priests hurried to her side and helped her to rise. She remembered that Jesus was called Yeshua at home and she asked for him. She whispered, and the young monk thought she was ill and tired out. He fetched Jesus, who came and gave her his hand. He asked if she needed help. Then she took off the hood, shook out her black hair, and rubbed the soot from her cheeks.

"'I have travelled all the way from Palestine to see you!' she said. 'I have much to tell you about the people at home.'

"That made Jesus happy. How unsuspecting men are! You don't suspect what is hidden in the mind of a woman in love: lies and deceit, as well as love and worship. Jesus really was happy. He asked Mary from Bethany to meet him in Alexandria the following evening.

"At first, the meeting was a happy reunion. Mary had made herself as pretty as she could, and she stole into his arms with shivering expectancy. When Jesus noticed her intimate caresses he was at first angry and then terribly disappointed. He pushed her off and asked mildly why she had come. She couldn't keep silent, and her violent emotions made her say something very silly. She said that now, as he had sent his wife away, she wanted to be his partner in everything. They had known each other since childhood, so she must mean a lot to him.

"Jesus listened, and fended off her advances. He asked about his mother, about her sister and brother, and other mutual friends. She answered his questions, but went on talking about her love for him and her unhappy marriage. Jesus knew Samuel and felt quite sorry for him. He rose and told Mary that he was not interested to be anything but the good friend he had always been to her. Moreover, he thought she should go back to Samuel and try to be a good wife. Samuel was a good man and did not deserve to be deceived.

"Mary returned to Palestine and to her brother and sister. But she was never herself again and did not go back to Samuel. In the meantime her brother Lazarus had married and his wife could not stand Mary. There were repeated conflicts, and Martha had a hard time being the conciliator. Lazarus died – this time for real – and Mary left the house. There are no traces of her after that."

"That was a sad story, Lydia," I confirmed. "The traces of Jesus ended in Heliopolis. Do you know if he died there?"

"Jesus was 183 years old when he died!" Lydia answered. "I know it is difficult to believe, but you seek the Truth. He knew he would have a long life, and his mission did not end in Heliopolis. He stayed there until he was 100 years old. After that he wandered. He was wandering around in China, India and Tibet, and many other places. He founded monasteries and converted people, and in some strange way he was invulnerable."

"He must have had good legs," I added dryly. "I don't think we'll do any peep-holes to that time. What's next?"

"Quite a lot, Jan. Do you want to find out what happened to Jesus' children? Shall we go to southern Gaul again? There is the matter in dispute that Mary Magdalene stayed there and lived in a cave. I believe it is time to find out how it really was. But she lived in a cave, I guarantee you that. You probably would like to see more from that time."

"I would love to."

Said and done.

31. The Suffragette in the Cave

It was wonderful to come back to Gaul – or France, as it is called today. The almond trees were flowering, the whole region was flowering, the sea was radiantly blue, and the heavens were free from clouds. I always felt a weakness for France. Do not think that it is only because of the good wine. No, I always felt I knew France and the temperament of the French people and that I could adapt easily to living there. When the French are happy, they show it. Their exhilaration and child-like joy is like a singing wind. If they feel sad, they beat their breasts with sorrow and crawl on their knees to the triptych in the church and ask the Virgin for help. If they are angry – God help you!

We were standing on the quay in Massilia, looking at the throng of swarming people and boats, listening to cries, laughter, and song. We were materialized. I felt satisfied. Again I would feel the sweet wine of southern Gaul caress my tongue with its aromatic glow. Lydia read my thoughts and winced.

"Are we going to the Roman house?" I asked, happy to rejoin all the friends there.

"Mary Magdalene is no longer there," Lydia answered. "She moved to the cave when she got alone. Her daughter Sarah is married and lives in another town. So stop thinking of wine. We have more important things to investigate."

We had quite a long way to walk, but I enjoyed the great beauty of the landscape and the gentle winds that came from the waves in the harbor of Massilia. We walked up the Artemis mountain, where the image of the Greek goddess represents the Woman and the Mother. The cave is up high, with an incomparable view over this lovely, yet wild, landscape with its lushness, its blossoming, and its balsamic scents.

I was expecting a cave which looked like the ones I have seen before, with damp walls, damp floor, stalactites and stalagmites, and water running everywhere. This one was different.

For certain, a brook with crystal clear water ran through it. Yet the innermost part of the cave was converted into a comfortable home. One part was a bedroom, one part a kitchen, and the rest a big living room. In one corner there was, to my surprise, a hand-loom. Behind it a figure appeared that I recognized as Mary Magdalene. She certainly was older, and there were wrinkles in her handsome face, but her smile was still characterized by rare beauty. That smile had charmed and converted so many to the teachings of Jesus. She was dressed in a loose gray dress, and her dark-red hair, slightly streaked with gray, was plaited with lilac ribbons.

"If my eyes serve me right," she exclaimed, "I see my old friends Lydia and Jan from the Angelic Realm. Welcome!" She ran to us and hugged us both, and I saw tears of joy in her eyes. "You are as young and pretty as last time," she sighed. "I am aging in my loneliness. Sarah lives far from here, and my friends Nicodemus and Maximin and the others are dead. I have done my share, Jan! I am tired now. Silence is my best friend nowadays, when I don't have my dear disciples around me. My heart tells me to continue to teach them, even if they are not so many nowadays."

"Are they young men?" I asked.

"No, they're mostly women." Mary Magdalene smiled. "I've always stood up for my fellow sisters."

"I can see you are weaving," said Lydia, looking at the tapestry on the loom. It shimmered in the loveliest colors.

"It is a luxury I still permit myself," Mary said, smiling. "I weave my dreams into the cloth; that's why it shimmers. When I am no longer here, my daughter will have the loom and all the clothes that I have woven. It is a very strong message to her."

"People say that you don't eat or drink anymore," said Lydia. Mary laughed and showed us the little stream that calmly flowed through the cave room. Then she showed us a fireplace further away.

"I have as much water as I like," she continued. "And of course I eat. I am quite satisfied with what Nature gives me, and there is plenty on the mountain and all around here: leaves, roots, berries, fruits, and nuts. Sometimes I bake bread, and often my disciples bring me bread and other necessities. I'm well provided for. I like living like this. People tire me out. Don't you sometimes feel that way too?"

"Yes." I smiled. "People can be very tiresome, especially those who are greedy for power and money. But please tell us what has happened since we were together in Heliopolis."

We sat down on some skins that were laid in front of the fireplace. Mary made a little fire and then she began telling us, "Sarah was very emotionally influenced by the trip to Heliopolis. It was the last time she saw her father. We know that he is alive; I sometimes get letters from him and I often write to him. He says that when he has completed his mission in Heliopolis he will go on wanderings and then it will be more difficult to have any contact. But by that time I will probably no longer be on Earth, and then I will await him in a higher world.

"My faithful friend Hannah stayed with me, and she was the one who mostly brought up Sarah. Maximin taught my daughter to read, write, count, and think. The thinking wasn't the less important, it was her innermost that now and then must be purified. I travelled a lot. When Maximin didn't travel with me, there were always other young, dedicated disciples at hand. I was never alone, and I had lots of proposals and declarations of love. The women were more insecure, but it normally worked out when I assembled them and talked to them as if they were my sisters. When I came home I always was struck with wonder when I saw how Sarah had grown and developed during my absence. At that time I didn't reproach myself. The repentance and the reproaches came later on. I felt as if I always wandered around in a long cloak with the hood stowed. I didn't realize that I had missed the most important thing that life gives to a woman: my child."

"Why are you not with her now?" I ventured to ask.

"She will not forgive me. I am not allowed to see my grandchildren, nor share my dreams with my one beloved child."

One child? I remembered David, but I didn't know if I was allowed to ask. In that case Lydia should tell her that he was alive. Wasn't it enough, with all the sorrow that Mary Magdalene already carried inside? And what could Mary Magdalene actually do about that now? He was in the monastery at Lake Garda, among Christian monks who at this time had an uneven struggle against the heathen.

"Are you going to die here alone, without seeing either your son or your daughter again?" I asked coldly. "That's unforgivable egotism. How can a mother refrain from at least trying to ask for forgiveness? Don't you want to meet your grandchildren? Are you trying to convince yourself that mourning a man who isn't even dead is your life task from now on? What do you think your son David thinks of you, far away in that Essene monastery? He has probably forgotten that he ever had a mother." Lydia stared in astonishment at me.

Mary Magdalene started to weep. She went to the brook and washed her face in the clear water. After that she looked at us in grief.

"Please leave my cave," she asked. "I'm in contact with loving Angels who help me all the time. I don't want Jan to tell me what to do. I thought you knew better than that. I forgive you, but please, don't ever come back here."

Lydia was very angry with me when we left the cave. "You did it again," she reproached me. "You interfered with history. You committed a terrible blunder."

I immediately turned around and returned. When I entered the cave, Mary was sitting staring into space with tears slowly running down her cheeks.

"I don't want to leave you like this," I said, and took her hands. "No offence was intended. You must forgive my clumsiness. I thought I was helping you, but I was very wrong. You must know what ruffians men can be!"

Now she smiled, dried her eyes, and hugged me. I felt an approving Lydia behind me.

"I do forgive you," Mary Magdalene said. "I believe I felt angry, because you were right. I will think it over. Would you like to share some fruit and bread with me?"

We did. When we were there I obtained information about Mary Magdalene that I hadn't known, or even suspected. She had accomplished a life's work that probably no one who has portrayed her life has known about. I suddenly realized that in this simple cave lived a woman who was unique. She was not only the love and confidante of Jesus, but also the very first woman to advocate feminism. In short: a splendid suffragette! I let her speak about it:

"How do you think the women of our time feel? Nowadays contempt for women is spread out in most countries. It is a snake, a cobra that raises its head and hisses in all directions: 'Don't approach me, because I am a man. Obey, and have a good time. Disobey, and you will be severely punished.' So many men maltreat their women. Of course, there are good and loving men here as well as dominant women who make sure they are treated properly. But alas, not many of that kind exist. Women are born to be men's slaves. They preferably should give birth to boys, not girls. Girls are circumcised as an act of submission to a master. Women are untalented in all areas except for pleasing a man. I think all this has been dictated by evil itself.

"I have worked with women all my life. It was more difficult in Palestine than here. I met much resistance in Jerusalem, but here it was easier after I'd met Sarah, the gypsy queen. I learned a lot from her. I went out and preached. I assembled women and talked to them. I have a faithful group of women who still follow me. Many of them will carry on the feminist movement after my death."

"I thought you preached the same as Jesus." I was surprised that she didn't. Lydia laughed up her sleeve.

"Oh yes, I did that too. But now I mostly try to support women. That means that I encourage their courage and their desire to learn the same things as men. The ones who want this come to my cave. There are no protesting men standing around us here, like they do in the markets. We perform our tasks, but we also want the chance to go further and study. Men are frightened when they find out I have studied, whereas women admire my courage. I try to tell them that not only courage is necessary, but also the will not to remain a slave, not to only give birth to children and to cook. My father was the first one to encourage me." Now tears again were running down her cheeks.

"I didn't want to disturb my son. He would be ashamed of me if he knew I preach for the women. I don't think they would let me in into the monastery. What do you think?"

I gave her no answer, and just hugged her. The suffragette in the cave, I thought. A figurehead for the freedom of women! It was a solemn thought, near to ecstasy. A woman for the women, equal to men in the first century of our era, and nobody has ever noticed this. It was actually something much more important than becoming a saint!

When we left the cave for the second time after an interesting chat with our hostess – who was to be a saint – Lydia said, "You will not meet Mary Magdalene any more. Now we have other Truths to find. But I wonder, Jan, if you understand us women thoroughly? The most common thing is that we constantly walk around with a bad conscience. That makes us angry sometimes. We feel the pressure from our environment, demands and expectations we cannot meet or have the energy to fulfill. To demand something from someone else is difficult, and when we do, we often tread on his or her toes. We must refrain from demanding things and refrain from having bad opinions of people."

"But don't you think, too, that the lady in the cave ought to go out and look at the world again?" I asked. "Without any demands, just because she wants to. Meet her children and be happy with them?" Lydia nodded, and the dimples in her cheeks deepened.

"She actually did, later on," she answered. "Maybe our visit had some effect after all."

At home, in the Angelic Realm, I sat down for a moment outside my house in the little garden where the apple trees were blooming. Was it spring? I very well knew that what I saw was a chimera, a kind of holographic safety for me. Lydia sat down at my side. I looked at her soft profile and asked, "Who are you, Lydia?"

32. Lydia's Story

"Last time I was born on Earth was in England," Lydia said. "My father was a doctor, first in London and then district medical officer in Wales. My mother bore him eight children, but two of them died of scarlet fever. I was the third child, with three brothers and two sisters. My father liked living in a small village in this legendary landscape and my mother had her hands full with us kids. I was born at the beginning of the twentieth century.

"Life in the country was calm and peaceful, except that there were sick people and sick cattle, both inside and outside of my father's district. I worked a lot when I was growing up. I took care of my younger siblings and I was taken care of by the older ones. There was not much time to play, but Father was a cheerful and humorous person and we loved to be with him when he came home. He always joked and played with us. Mother was very strict.

"I had a secret friend. This friend was the enemy of my mother, and my father called her a funny witch. She was an old woman who lived on the outskirts of the village. Before we came, when the village was still very small, she had been the only one who could give medical care to the villagers. Many villagers visited her, even after we arrived. I met her in the woods when I was looking after my little three-year-old brother. I got fiercely interested in her amazing skills. She taught me about medicinal herbs and many other things. But most of all, I liked when she talked about old times. She had an inexhaustible store of stories. It was this knowledge that later made me a scientist in religious history.

"At first, my sisters and brothers and I went to the village school to learn to read and write. After that, we all were sent to different places for further study. I was sent to an uncle and aunt in London with one of my younger brothers. I was ten years old. For the first time in my life

I experienced human evil. Just as my father was lively and humorous, so my uncle was gloomy and uptight. His wife was totally subdued. She huddled up, cast down her eyes and said, 'Yes, Dick dear' or 'No, Dick dear.' I never heard many other words from her. But my uncle had dark designs on me. I didn't realize what he intended. But soon I became the victim of an outrage.

"I didn't dare to say anything in the beginning, because my uncle threatened me. He said he would kill me if I mentioned a single word about it. The second time when he came into the room where my little brother and I slept, I started to scream. My aunt came into the chamber, and I saw in her face that she knew what was going on, but she didn't say a word. She left the room, and my uncle completed his terrible deed. But the next morning my aunt gave me a small amount of money. 'Go home, children,' she said, and that was what we did.

"When we got home I told the truth to my parents. My father examined me, and he looked livid. I had only seen my dad angry when we were disobedient, but this time he was furious, in a real rage. The next day he went to London, and I suspect my uncle was taught a lesson he would never forget.

"It was just me and my younger brother at home now, in addition to the two smallest boys. Mother gave us lessons in geography, history, and other subjects. I was very interested in history and borrowed all books I could get hold of from the library. I read the Bible from cover to cover and I was gifted with a rather unusual memory. All I read was filed into compartments in my head. At last Dad realized that I had to study. He sent me to a school in London. There I took some tests, which I successfully passed. The headmaster of the school advised me to read history in order to become a historian.

"My schoolmates dreamed and talked of boys, but I only dreamed of all the thrilling adventures in history, especially in religious history. But this didn't help. A marriage was threatening, and I was more or less tricked into it. I met a boy at a friend's dinner party. He was an officer, and before I could say 'Jack Robinson' I was married to him. He was my first love, apart from my infatuation for the emperor Claudius or the disciple John the Beloved, whom I imagined as a dark-eyed romantic.

"I was disappointed. At first it was wonderful, but after a few months things changed. I became pregnant and started to put on weight. My husband didn't like that. He started drinking, and when he was drunk he beat me. The same old story. I gave birth to our daughter Ophelia, and my husband didn't even come to see us at the hospital. We divorced. I went home to my parents in Wales with my little daughter and stayed there during her first year of life. It was fun, but it was hard work. I studied as much as I could, I spent all my free time with Ophelia, and I also helped my mother as much as I could. My dad, who meant more and more to me, didn't like my situation. He was my confidant and the only one to understand me. He thought that I was wasting my talents in a forgotten village in Wales.

"Without my knowing it, Dad arranged for my future and my career through friends in London. I started at the high school for teachers in Eaton, Chester, and could at last devote myself to my passion: religious history. I discovered a lot of shortcomings, defects, misunderstandings, and gaps in historical religious books, not least in the Bible. They didn't agree with each other and they said different things.

"I made remarks and comments; I wrote articles and studied all the time from morning until night. Meanwhile, my parents took care of my little daughter. We never heard from her father, neither did he give me any alimony, which was commonly occurring at that time. My father helped me and managed to find a lawyer, who forced my ex-husband to pay an amount of money to me each month. In this way the years passed by.

"When Ophelia was seven, I fell in love for the second time. At that time I was already a well-known religious historian, who had to appear in the media out in the big world. This time the object of my feelings was a rich, distinguished businessman who had been married before. He had two teenagers. I had to change my life totally, but Love is a demanding rascal! My husband was not interested in religious history, and he had a palace in the noble business world of London. Ophelia and I moved in. Ophelia was now known as Offy.

"I didn't want to give up my career for the sake of love. I did not fit in as a charming hostess in a charming home with my charming step-children. I started to study again after a year as a bored luxury-wife. My husband didn't like it, so he presented me an ultimatum. He wanted me to go with him on a two-month cruise to the South Sea Islands. I couldn't resist. But if I still preferred religious history to him when we returned, we would divorce.

"I really loved my husband, even if we were different. We had so many common interests. Both of us loved adventures and unknown, alien, exciting experiences. We started a strange journey that took us to our final destination: death. I found out that I wanted to write a book about my controversial thoughts concerning the Bible and other things. My husband agreed and even encouraged me.

"We were in Polynesia, and one of the harbors was at Tahiti. This was in the 1950s, after the Second World War. I have not told you about the war; you wanted to know my private story, didn't you? Our boat was anchored in the harbor for a couple of days and we wanted to see whales, so we hired an old fisherman with a small fishing boat. He was eager to have us on board, so we hired him for a day, together with an American couple. That was our destiny. A sudden storm ended all our lives and the fishing boat.

"That's my life in a nutshell. I never knew my daughter Offy as a grown-up. But here I am experiencing something else. My thoughts are not as controversial as before. Like you, I always wanted to know the Truth."

"And you are a very sensible person compared to stormy Jan," I laughed. "But now it's time for the next peep-hole. I always wondered what happened to John, the brother of James. Where did he go after the Crucifixion?"

"Okay, let's find out now!" said Lydia, and suddenly I closed my eyes. She took my hand. The flight, or whatever you call it, didn't last long.

33. John the Beloved Leaves Patmos

"We are now on Patmos in the Greek islands," Lydia told me. "John the Beloved has been here in exile for a year and a half. We will visit him now."

Behind us, the sea gurgled upon the white sand. We saw rugged, naked cliffs without much vegetation bordering the shores. We were visible, since I could see Lydia clearly outlined against the gray rock. She had a long white dress and a golden ribbon in her hair. A dark Spanish cloak was thrown over her shoulders. I looked at myself. I had the same old monk's habit as usual. That was obviously my uniform for peep-holes.

A path wound its way among the cliffs. The path was bordered with waving marram grass, and after a short while we reached a settlement. There was a high wall, and behind it a small town. We went through a gate in the wall. We could see tall buildings, streets, and a market. It looked all bare and dull, without trees or flowers. Lydia guided me easily, as if she had been there before. Later she told me that she always walks solely on intuition. She finds without searching. Everybody ought to know how to do it, practically and symbolically: to find without searching.

The town had a church-like building. We went inside. An elderly man rose from his kneeling position as we approached the altar. I realized that it must be John the Beloved. His round face was lined, but with good features, and his dark brown eyes were clear and sharp. His eyebrows were black and his hair was dark brown, but he had many white hairs. He smiled to us, revealing a line of beautiful white teeth. When he smiled, his whole person was alight, and you felt warmth and love coming from him.

"You are welcome here!" he exclaimed. "I can see you come from afar!" As usual, we told him we were Angels from the Angelic Realm who were looking for the Truth.

"Everyone's truth is a truth for themselves," was his cryptic answer. He showed us to an inner room of the building. The furnishings were spartan, but very beautifully embroidered tapestry hung on the walls. There were several low stools with pretty cushions. On an altar-like table were two tall candlesticks with wax candles.

"The truth you seek may not be valid for all people," he continued. "There are many worlds and many truths, you see. I understand you have come to see what happened to me after the Crucifixion. I have doubted, dear children, I have doubted!"

Lydia and I looked at each other in astonishment. John put his face in his hands, and when he took them away we saw tears in his eyes.

"Maybe it is too late to doubt afterwards," he said. "Doubt also contains truth or it would be impossible to doubt. I have wondered if I just followed the stream – or not. A leaf is thrown down the waterfall through the whirlpool and out into the sea. But before it comes to the sea it must either try to land or drown. That's how I felt. In young people the flame burns with a consuming power. It will extinguish when you grow older, and it may die. In my case it never did, but I assure you, I have doubted."

"Are you talking about Jesus?" I asked. He nodded.

"I questioned," he answered. "Love for another person can make you blind. I was rather blind, but I have fervently studied the knowledge he gave us and the knowledge I carry inside me, which maybe I've always had."

"Aren't they the same thing?" I asked.

"Yes and no," was the answer. "Life brings wisdom, but at first we don't notice it. Insight comes as we grow older – hopefully. I was deported to this island, and to begin with I thought it was unbearable. Then I started to look at myself. Who was I, really? I realized that I was like that leaf carried along by the flowing water and now I was heading for the shore. I landed on moss-covered earth, but it was my earth. It was my leaf on my earth and I could calmly walk further. The next step will be Ephesus, and I won't go any further. I will be a trumpet there, a trumpet that preaches. Not everyone will listen, but many will hear the call and walk with me."

"Have you written the Gospel of John yet?" asked Lydia.

The prophet seemed startled. "I haven't written a gospel and I won't," was his angry answer. "Why should I?"

"Well, it's in the Bible, anyhow," I interposed, to save Lydia.

"And what is the Bible, if I may ask?" John asked suspiciously.

"Something that will be of great importance in the future," I answered. "The Gospel of John tells the story of Jesus."

"I wonder who wrote it," John pondered, rubbing his chin. Then he gave a start and smiled with a smile that must always charm his listeners.

"You know, if the disciples wrote down the story of Jesus, there would be as many stories as disciples. I believe the stories would not be the same at all. People see things very differently and here we are, my friends: here is this thing about the Truth. I have finished looking for it. I talk the way the wind blows and the way the sun caresses my body, because I talk with my heart, not with my head. It's the heart that must be developed first. The head can always learn a lesson, but the heart has no lessons."

"You say wise things," Lydia agreed. "When do you leave here?"

"You arrived at the last moment." John patted her hand. "I'm leaving here tomorrow, dear," he said. "What about coming with me to Ephesus?"

Lydia looked at me and nodded, and I answered quickly, "If you want us to go with you, dear Master, it would be an honor. What time does the boat leave?"

Early the following morning at sunrise we were on the boat, which was sailing from the harbor of Patmos, with Ephesus as its destination. On board were John the Beloved, Lydia, and I, but also some of his disciples. Another adventure was waiting for us, I thought, and stretched out beside the older man. Lydia was standing a bit further away at the rail and saw the small Greek island Patmos disappear behind the horizon. Asia Minor waited for us!

The magnificent seaport Ephesus, which was on the estuary of the river Kaystro, appeared to us through the sweeping clouds of mist the morning we arrived. It was an impressive sight. I had never before reflected upon antique building structure, but now I was astonished. In my last life on Earth we used the word "modern" to mean something that was not old-fashioned, something we could be proud of because it was new and nice. Now I was in the Asia Minor of ancient history and had been expecting it to be an undeveloped country.

"Well, Jan," said a voice behind me. "This doesn't look bad, does it? I think there will be many who need to hear the Truth." This was followed by a good-natured laugh that I had learned to love and enjoy during the boat trip. John had sent his friends in advance, who would arrange accommodation for us. I looked forward to going ashore in this famous harbor.

34. John's Mission in Ephesus

The temple of the fertility goddess Artemis was a noteworthy sight, even for a spoiled Angel. It had 127 columns and was gigantic. Unfortunately, the Goths would destroy it a couple of hundred years later. In this marvelous city there was also the biggest ancient theater of the time, with room for 50,000 spectators. John walked around with a proud smile on his face and showed us also the magnificent and comprehensive library. The big city library in Stockholm would disappear beside this one, I thought. In "modern times" there is no such elegant architecture to be found.

The wisest, most wonderful human being I've ever met through history was walking at my side, arm in arm with Lydia. He entertained us with legends and historical facts from old Ephesus. His stories were told with wisdom and a good portion of subtle comments. A wise man with eyes glittering with humor, I thought.

"You must learn how to differentiate knowledge from wisdom," he said suddenly, as if he had read my thoughts (perhaps he had!). "Knowledge is something you learn, wisdom is something you have in your heart, but also in cellular memories from past lives that we all carry with us. We live many lives in order to learn and develop more and more. In every life there is wisdom available if we recognize it, but we also have our free will. Our free will can destroy, annihilate, but also improve us."

"What would have happened if we had no free will?" asked Lydia.

"We would have been slaves to something else," was the answer. "We need our free will, even if we can't handle it. But we can learn to manage it, so that the will is our slave and not the opposite. When this is the case it can perform miracles. We need it in order to learn to control matter."

"What do you mean, John?" I asked. His words were very intriguing. "Control matter? Are we magicians or alchemists, without knowing it?"

"We all have hidden potentials that we don't use," answered the former apostle. "It will not be until your time, or perhaps later, when we learn how to use them. Before that, inventions have been made that will change the world and that may destroy man. Sometimes when I look into the future I get quite frightened."

"Some scriptures from my time say that you came here with Jesus' mother Mary, and that she is buried here," I remarked.

"That's true," John answered. "I made my last trip to Ephesus with Mary. We both felt that Jesus somehow failed us by being crucified. Why couldn't he, who possessed so much more spiritual power than us ordinary mortals, prevent the Crucifixion? Why was he hanging there, weak and bleeding instead of thundering and flashing and frightening his enemies?

"Believe me, my head was full of questions, and his mother and Mary from Bethany were thinking along the same lines. By the way, how could that young woman have the courage to stay through the whole Crucifixion? Jesus had sent his wife, Mary Magdalene, away in order to save her from all this. Jesus was obsessed by the idea that he would save the people by being crucified and that way get his teachings known everywhere. That was what he said to me. I and many of the other disciples tried to persuade him to refrain from this voluntary death.

"Some of us also knew that this death wasn't real, in spite of his sufferings, and that he would be in a coma when he was taken down from the cross. He forbade us to say a word about this. I'm breaking my silence now, because he is not my leader any more. He informed some of us that we would meet a couple of times before he vanished for good. And when he vanished, we were not allowed to look for him. Jan, I know that he is still alive and that you are keeping your mouth shut on my behalf. You don't have to. I am free now, free to teach my Truth."

I told John that Jesus was living in Heliopolis and that he was strong and well. He listened carefully and I saw tears of joy in his eyes.

I also told him of my travels with Mary Magdalene, the birth of Sarah, and how David was hidden in an Essene monastery. After that, John hugged us both and breathed a deep sigh of relief.

"I will tell you about Mother Mary," he said, when we had our first meal together in Ephesus. We found ourselves in a nice little house that I don't know how he had gotten hold of. It seemed like he had many friends here from former times.

"We came here directly after the Crucifixion," he went on. "I came here to preach, and I preached the teachings of Jesus! So did Mary. She was like a mother to me, and that was also Jesus' wish. We converted many people in this city and in the countryside. We wandered a lot. At last, it was too much for Mary. She didn't know that her son was alive, even if she maybe anticipated it. Her health was faltering and I was planning to return to Galilee with her, but she didn't want to. If you like we can visit her grave tomorrow."

The following day, when we were standing in front of Mother Mary's grave, John was silent at first. He put his hands over the grave and I realized he blessed it. I bowed and Lydia kneeled devoutly, and I saw she was deeply moved. We slowly walked the narrow road back to town between the many poplars.

"Do you know something, my children?" John said, and put his hands on our shoulders. He walked between us and looked first into my eyes, then Lydia's. "No, you cannot know that I didn't worship Jesus from the beginning. I worshipped John the Baptist and was one of his most devoted disciples. I was young, still a teenager at that time, and he was my idol. The man in the rough gray camelhair cloak, the man with wild black curls and burning eyes, which could etch themselves into you like sharp, piercing spears, was to me the incarnation of devotion to God, purity, and penance. He was an impressive man, a great Master and redeemer.

"Later, when I got to know the man, the friend and the child's father, I got very surprised. I followed him to his cave, I got acquainted with his lovely woman and his three children. All the time I wondered who he really was. 'I am a forerunner,' he often repeated. 'I am a forerunner of the Messiah, the son of God and the redeemer of humanity.' I, who thought that this fantastic man was a redeemer, didn't understand how he could claim that he was clearing the way for another redeemer. What could be more important, more pure, and more beautiful than the words of John the Baptist? I actually decided to dislike that son of God who would come soon. What do you say about that, my dear children?"

Again John's white teeth sparkled in a big, warm smile. Lydia laughed loudly but my smile was a little uncertain. I had not expected this. I always imagined the apostle John the Beloved hanging around Jesus like a dog wanting to be cuddled and also jealous of the family life of his idol. Now John's smile turned into a joyous laughter which shook his whole body. Either he read my thoughts or Lydia worked magic to make the thoughts appear inside his head. Sometimes she was a little joker.

"Well," resumed John, after drying his tears, "I decided to find out about this mystic cousin. When Jesus was baptized, I was standing in the background, but I only saw a humble young man, who looked nice and friendly. My leader, friend, and Master baptized this young man. Could that really be the famous Jesus? I saw a pretty girl standing on the shore, waving to him. I saw that Jesus smiled at her. But it was also a strange atmosphere out there in the water. The Sun behaved in a funny way. It shone very vividly around the Baptism, and also Mary Magdalene had a kind of halo of light around her for a short moment. I understood that something tremendous was happening, and people all around were unusually silent and still. It was as if time stood still, as if the whole world had stopped."

"Haven't you written about it?" asked Lydia.

"The only things I have written about are my visions. I wrote about them on Patmos, because there I experienced strange things. I have brought them here, needless to say. Maybe I will write something more in the future; we'll see."

"Have you never been married?" Lydia asked him.

John stopped. He raised his hands as if in prayer. Then he asked silently, "How did you know? Do Angels know all about people? Well,

I will tell you about my life. Maybe it's beneficial both for you and for me. I have thought a lot during my imprisonment on Patmos. Actually it was good for me."

"Another question first," I hastened to say. "It says in the Bible that when you and Mother Mary were standing at the foot of the cross, Jesus said, 'Mother, see your son, and son, see your mother!' Didn't Mary and Joseph have many children? Did you not have your own parents?"

It took until evening before I got an answer to that question. He first wanted to show us the attractions of the beautiful city. We viewed an amazing theater and after that an equally amazing library. Speaking of modern! During our "modern" times no such thing is built. We went on a marvelous sight-seeing tour until the Sun was wandering towards the moment of shadow and it was time to return to the nice little house in the outskirts of Ephesus. After a delightful evening meal, served by some women who belonged to the parish John had founded at his first visit here, we had the chance of a chat.

"You must not go back to the future without hearing the Truth about me," John began. "I am not at all interested in your Bible. From what I understand, no living author, but Luke, has contributed anything to it. My friends and companions from the time with Jesus have had different destinies, but unfortunately they are already dead. The cruel persecutions of the Romans have hit them. I am happy enough to have made it this far. There are a few of us who were close to Jesus, and we are the only ones who can tell the Truth. So please try to believe me now, Jan and Lydia."

"It's like a puzzle, and we're putting it together piece by piece," I answered. "You are alive, but so are Jesus and Mary Magdalene. The New Testament of our Bible goes up in smoke. We want to know where that smoke is derived. There is a red thread of historical events that we recognize, but we have no foundation, nothing to really lean on."

John nodded thoughtfully and then continued his story. "My father was a fisherman called Zebedee. My mother's name was Salome, which like Mary is a common name in Palestine. We were poor, but we had a decent life. We lived near the lake of Gennesareth, not far from

Capernaum. My brother James, who was much older than me, had already joined Father fishing when I was a small boy. My mother was a loving woman, caring and full of empathy, although we sometimes lived on almost nothing. I also had three sisters.

"The change came when I met John the Baptist. James never became his disciple, but I gave up fishing and followed John instead. I was only fifteen at the time. My understanding mother convinced my father that it was only a passing whim that I would get over soon enough. Moreover, there would now be one mouth less to feed back home. I would rather starve with John the Baptist than with my family at home.

"I learned a lot during my time with John. There was an old man versed in the Scriptures who admired John the Baptist and who followed him wherever he went. That old man taught me to read and write. I had no difficulties in learning. I had always admired knowledge, and now I received it. I knew my parents wanted me to marry, and I was present at my brother James' wedding. That was before I met Jesus. There I met a beautiful girl who was the daughter of a vineyard worker. I fell in love and we were betrothed. Her name was Elisa. She was fair-haired and blue-eyed and had a smiling mouth. She had dimples in her rosy cheeks. In short, she represented my vision of an Angel.

"I went back to the Baptist, though, before my parents could prevent me. The betrothal was still ongoing. My mother told Elisa that I would soon be back. I did come back, but not until John was beheaded. Then I was comforted by my faithful fiancée. We married. I was still very young, and so was she. It was a matter of honor for a young man to marry, or he would not be counted as a man. That was the custom at that time, and I imagine that it's still the case today.

"My father wanted me to start fishing again. I didn't want to. Now I could read and write, and I hoped for a career as a scribe. At that time, Jesus Christ came into my life. He also came into James' life. It changed everything. As long as Jesus stayed near Gennesareth we could be with our families, but we left them when we were travelling with him. When I came back from the first trip with Jesus, there was terrible news. We had walked from Capernaum to Bethsaida and back again. When I came home I hurried to our house to greet my wife, who was pregnant. My beloved Elisa was dead.

"She had died in childbirth, but given birth to a little girl. The child was alive, but my mother was not sure she would make it. She was baptized Myriam. The red, wrinkled baby did not interest me. I escaped from everything in order to travel with Jesus and be with the other disciples. Remember, dear friends, I was only twenty, and not mature enough to be responsible for my family. My mother took care of the baby. I didn't ask if my child would live or die.

"Jesus comforted me in my sorrow. He assured me that my daughter was in good hands, and now the time had come to devote all my powers and all my thinking to the good Father. I was free to devote my life to the preaching of the holy wisdom. At that time I believed him, but I don't know if I do now. He liberated me from the responsibility to take care of my own daughter. I know that she survived, that she grew up to be a beautiful girl, and that she married early. I also know she married a good man. Myriam lives in my home country and has a good life without me."

"You know that she lives in Palestine?" Lydia interrupted. "Why have you not contacted her?"

"If I do, the Romans will catch me again. They know which disciples Jesus had, and who the survivors are. I think she has to live her life in peace. I have heard that she has at least five children. Shall I expose them to persecution? Myriam would not even recognize me, and what could we talk about? A sea of emotions would throw its breakers between us – to what end? I have a mission here, and I want to complete it."

"I think you are a calmer prophet than the Baptist and Jesus," I mused.

"Sometimes you have to roar," said John, smiling. "Lions are needed, but not for killing martyrs. I am not a penitent, I am a teacher. I want to make people free from idolatry and ancient, terrible, heathen customs. I want Love."

"Please define the word Love. How do you interpret it?" asked Lydia.

"There are so many kinds of love," answered John. "Love between yin and yang, between parents and children, is not what you're asking about, is it? Love for Nature is part of a far greater Love that rises from the earth and sea. It opens out into a tremendous bell, which picks up the music of the spheres. It rings out across the infinite universe. Somewhere in those worlds the Power we call God lives. That Power is our Father and Mother. That Power is pure, unconditional Love. Inside that Power we stop wondering; we don't ask. That's our home, that's where we belong, isn't it, Angels?"

"It's a bit more complicated than that," I answered, "but that is how far people can understand. That's the most important. But now tell me about the mother and the son, that is, Jesus' mother and you."

"I did not understand it myself when we knelt in front of the cross," John answered. "Between you and me, I believe that Jesus was a little confused at that moment. Maybe he meant that he wanted me to take care of his mother Mary after his so-called death, and so I did. Joseph had died many years ago. He died when Jesus was travelling. The other sons had their professions, and I don't know what they thought about their elder brother. They were born of the same womb, yet Jesus was a stranger to them. They probably didn't understand their mother either.

"I had heard of the heathen city Ephesus in Asia Minor, and it was not far away. There were people of many different nationalities there. It was a promising place for my work. I asked Mary to go with me, because I felt that she needed a change. She agreed, and we went to Ephesus. We stayed here for a few years and succeeded in assembling quite a few people. You have seen Mother Mary's grave today. When she died, I went back to Jerusalem and started to preach. A small group assembled around me, but it grew, and the Romans were afraid that my influence would be too great. That's when they sent me away to Patmos. Since I had not done anything evil, they didn't want to throw me to the lions. But they didn't know that I was a lion!"

Night had fallen while we were exploring John's thrilling life. The stars seemed very near. We went to bed with yet more questions, but they had to wait until the next day.

35. Philosophical Conversation with John

One piece at a time of the puzzle seemed to fit. It was a relief.

"You are making a new Bible!" Lydia joked the next morning, when we were eating a tasty breakfast in John's house. We were not alone. People came and went, some sat at the table, but John was not there yet.

"I don't know yet what's missing, but we have to find out," I whispered to Lydia. "We have to return home today, but I am sure there is something more John wants to tell us."

"The morning is pouring its gold over the lands! Let us take a last walk together. I know you must leave today."

John was standing behind us, and maybe he had heard me. It seemed that he heard with more than his ears. I believe that is just what a prophet does: He hears with more than his ears, he sees with more than his eyes, and he talks with more than his mouth. We rose and followed him out of the house. I will always remember him as I saw him that morning: He wore a violet cloak and he had a long golden staff with the head of a golden eagle at the top. We walked up a nearby mountain, where we had a marvelous view of the great harbor swarming with people.

"You have a staff with an eagle, and you say you are a lion," I joked. He smiled.

"I have learned some conjuring tricks," he answered. "I can be both eagle and lion when it is needed. The eagle means sharp-sightedness and magical power. The lion means attack and defense. That suits me, doesn't it?"

I nodded and smiled and he went on, "It feels slightly magical to talk about life with Angels. On the other hand I believe it was not long since you were in the middle of the pulsating streams called life. Do you long for a new life on Earth?"

We both shook our heads. He continued, "What I teach is named Christianity. It's not my idea, and it definitely doesn't come from Jesus. It is a name which will cause schism. Belief needs no name. Belief can be any belief, because we all have the right to believe, and nobody needs to jostle one another in the name of belief. What I fear is that when you christen and baptize people they implacably fall into a belief. Baptism is a nice tradition, but not something necessary for belief. The only thing needed is that deep inside you know a Higher Being exists, a Higher Power that brings safety and above all Love. You can build whatever you like around your faith, but I believe that every human ought to keep their own flame in their heart and not force anyone else to share that flame. If that was the case, there would be no foes or wars."

I listened to his words with awe. That was exactly what I thought. I was thinking about the small progress that had been made in the twentieth century when I lived on Earth. We had one foot in heathendom and the other in so-called Christianity. I guess the same applies to the twenty-first century, when my medium on Earth writes down my words. That part of the development has probably not changed much during the more than forty Earth-years I have spent with the Angels. But I soon heard even stranger words from our host:

"I live in what has been, in what is, and in what is to come. The only thing I wish from life right now is for my daughter to forgive me. I don't see the future as a big welcoming light, but as an expanse of vibrating darkness. Every lie that is told, which is the basis of the religion they call Christianity, will characterize the future. Abuse of power and filthy lucre will govern the world. No one will escape. Christianity will be the hell of a doctrine with that Bible book you mentioned. Maybe it will fade like a flame that burns out. I wish I could be spared seeing the future, but I must warn you and ask you to pass on the warning. Tell people to love each other. Make a knot of friendship all over the Earth. Always light a candle for the Truth."

"That's hardly an encouraging forecast for the world," I protested. "Good things will also happen."

"I dared to return to Ephesus because the Roman Emperor Nerva took the throne," answered John. "He is a good, but almost too mild, Emperor. He has not the iron hand that actually is needed. But for my part, I do well here. My Christian group is growing, as is my own experience of the people. But since I can look into the future, I know that Christianity will disappear from Asia Minor. Another prophet will be born, and his teaching will spread very quickly …"

"Mohammed," I interrupted. "He will be born in 500 years! You'd better write a gospel, after all, because John's gospel is in our Bible."

"I don't want to hear any more about your Bible!" John roared. "If I ever write something, it will be in my own way, and not a chapter in your Bible. But nevertheless, I understand that false prophets will build lies around the old scriptures that are to be found in Jerusalem and Alexandria.

"And now, my dear Angels, I can see that you have to leave. I would like you to come back in a couple of years, before I leave this life."

"We will make a new peep-hole as soon as we can." Lydia smiled and hugged John. He held her in his arms for a long time, and I saw he was moved. Then it was my turn to hug him and thank him for the outstanding cooperation. And I said "See you soon" and not "Farewell."

Lydia kept her promise. When we came back, she asked Kualli if we could visit John some years later. He said yes, and I will now tell you about that journey in connection with the first one.

This time we arrived right inside John's house. It seemed unchanged. Nobody sat on the pillared veranda, where myrtle and other unknown plants rustled and the wind whispered in the tops of the acacia trees. We stood there and enjoyed the silence, the scents, and the shimmering rose-colored evening light of the setting Sun.

"My dear Angels! I am so happy you came here right now. How wonderful to see you again!"

John was not alone. He had a woman at his side. She was obviously in her forties, and she was very beautiful. Her fair hair flew around her head and her big blue eyes were filled with love. She put her arm under the old prophet's arm. He had aged since the last time we saw him. His hair and beard were snow-white, but you couldn't miss the joy in his riddled face.

"My daughter Myriam has arrived!" he shouted happily. "My abandoned daughter has taken a ship across the great sea to meet her old father. And the best of all: She has forgiven me."

"That was not difficult." Myriam kissed her father's cheek. "I understand my father. But I haven't suffered. My grandmothers fought to take care of me, so I had it almost too good. I married a wonderful man and have five lovely children. I've had a good life, but I've missed my father all the time. A couple of years ago we started to write letters. Even if the letters took a long time to reach their destination, they became a foundation for understanding and forgiveness.

"I will soon return home with good news for my family," she continued. "Maybe Father will visit us in Capernaum. So you are the two Angels my father told me about?"

We had a lovely evening with an almost-exhilarated prophet and his pretty daughter. We enjoyed seeing him and listening to him once more.

"The best thing of all is forgiveness," he said. "To forgive yourself and others feels like a lava-stream through your body. It is rolling, warm and heavy, until it finds a spot where it can rest. Forgiveness is an elixir that everyone should drink. It has a connection with Love, because Love has so many faces, including joy. I never ceased to dream about the reunion of my daughter and myself. I sent joy across the gap that was between us. And look, a miracle happened!"

"I would like to talk more with you about Jesus Christ," I said. "You have doubted and believed. Which side are you on now?"

"On the foundation of absolute belief," he answered at once. "I have thought this through a thousand times; I have gone over things again and again. In his Sermon on the Mount, Jesus said that only four laws were needed in the life of a human: humility, care for others, the inner goodness of your heart, and to live righteously. I don't agree with him completely. There is more to it. To master your fear is extremely important, so important that you don't suspect the meaning of it. Fear breaks down a human and reduces him or her to a weak-minded, trembling cell."

"Nobody understands that in our time," Lydia interposed. "Everything is energy. Is it not possible to divide energy into different groups – for instance, positive and negative?"

"Yes. Energy is a very complex word that is misused in many contexts. I don't think Jesus explained sufficiently well what he meant by energy – moreover a word that he did not use. He talked about the Higher Self of the human."

"What is the relation between the Higher Self and the soul?" Myriam eagerly asked. I smiled because I knew the answer, but John responded.

"Your soul is in your Higher Self when you have left your Earth life. Your Higher Self is the new 'body' you get after death. I am rather an aspect, like you two are now, but time and space have played a trick on themselves to make us appear physically."

"Aspect?" I asked eagerly. "Is that the same thing as visual angle or perspective?"

"For me, an aspect is a relational inspiration," answered John.

"So we are relational inspirations sitting together chatting?" Lydia roared with laughter.

"Yes, you could say that." John smiled. "Jan, your medium on Earth has a relational source of inspiration in you. But let's not get lost in this hair-splitting. Let us enjoy ourselves for this short time. You will return home tomorrow, since you have new tasks waiting for you, dear Angels. Perhaps we shall go on from where we were last time you were here. Why I sometimes have doubted?"

"Yes, I never got an exhaustive answer to that," I said.

"Have you never doubted? Have you never thought: Does it have to be like this? It may well be a different way. That's why it is so important to have certain foundation stones and keep to them, like for instance Love, Joy, Forgiveness, Courage, etc. Jesus was brave, but I have often wondered why he was also foolhardy. It was not necessary for him to end up on the cross. He is descended from David, of course, but how many in our time aren't? It is a widespread dynasty. Can you really say that he has saved people, even in your time?"

"Not really," answered Lydia, "but he created a certain chaos!"

"Due to people's thirst for power and the ravages of Mammon." John's smile was very broad. "The word 'Christian' should never have been established. He should have known what he was up to. Of course, he didn't do it consciously. He meant well all the time, just like his cousin the Baptist. If the Baptist had been alive, I wonder what those two would have achieved together.

"Well, now it is I who have survived long and have tried to create a flow. I have dammed where it was necessary and made a waterfall where there were cliffs. Things have flowed calmly in most places. And now you can see reflections in the calm water. I hope it will continue like this, but I know it won't."

"Do you believe in reincarnation, John?" I asked.

"It is a Cosmic Law," he answered. "It's very natural, in my opinion. Of course, we must go back to Earth and develop through every life. I was the disciple of John the Baptist. He often said he had lived on Earth as the prophet Elijah. He taught me about reincarnation."

"What is the most important thing for you to tell us before we leave?" I asked.

"God," answered the old prophet. "God is the most important thing, the one and only gigantic Power that we call God. All other things follow in His footsteps. He is inside us and governing us all. Jan, you don't need to ask; you know where He is."

I nodded, and I smiled and thought about the eternal universe where the Great Spirit or God dwells and about all the other things I learned about Him on my earlier journeys. I would nevermore doubt, never ever!

"Shall we pray to God?" asked Lydia. "I mean is it better to turn to Him directly and not to Jesus or any other prophet?"

"Pray to whoever you like," said John, taking one of her hands in both of his. "I want everything that has to do with religion to be individual. At the same time, I revere God as the highest Spirit: the Father, the Mother, and the Son in one. You cannot separate yourselves from God, even if you want to. You are his creations. In the future, Jesus and God will be confused. Jesus will be an idol, worshipped by many. That's when the era of darkness begins.

"Jesus is a preacher like me, or the Baptist, or many others. His simulated death on the cross was a spurious signal. It wasn't his idea – it came from the whole posse who brought him back to life. I don't blame him, but if he had a choice, wouldn't he have chosen his Father's kingdom? I don't know if already on the cross he knew he would survive or if certain Essenes had prepared a rescue operation. They were expert doctors. I have been thinking a lot about this. People need an idol. Jesus played that part.

"In the future he will be called the Son of God and the cross will be his symbol. People talk about his death, and his death remains into the future. But wasn't it Christ that died on the cross and not Jesus? Isn't Jesus still alive and hiding in a monastery in Egypt? Why didn't he want to see us anymore, his faithful, loving disciples? I would like to know the role Judas played – staged by whom? Perhaps by Jesus? Judas cannot answer. He took his own life.

"If we asked him, do you think Jesus would answer these questions? He was the one who was never afraid, never gave way. But he kept his marriage to Mary Magdalene secret as long as possible. We didn't need to keep our marriages secret, but he insisted upon our attendance: to be with him, not with our families. I have thought deeply about this, dear Angels. I still love him, but it doesn't stop me from questioning his words and actions.

"It has gone too far already. Every human being has the energy of God inside, in every cell, and that is what brings us on. What Jesus taught us, and what I now try to preach, will be corrupted in the future. His name and God's name will be on banners of war. You Angels know about that; you come from a later age."

Of course we know, I thought. John's Truths are as relevant today as 2000 years ago. But still, the listening to and the learning of these Truths do not provide much result.

We continued to talk, while the face of the full moon looked down at us with its eternal smile. Myriam sat close to her father, with her head on his shoulder. The wind had died down and the air began to be chilly. It was time for Lydia and me to return to the Angelic Realm.

Both Lydia and I were rather shaken after our visit to John. He felt so real, so warm and sincere. His predictions were equal to the reality we both knew when we lived on Earth. Like other high Masters I had met, he put the possibilities and the solutions of all problems in the hands of humans. Certainly we can help each other – but are we doing so? Do we help ourselves, do we help each other, and do we thereby help God to map out our course of life in the right way? I don't think so.

John's doubts awakened many feelings, both in me and in Lydia. Had Jesus become a kind of idol who led to both good and evil? If evil people used his name, was that basically his fault? Questions, questions, questions that could not be answered. Maybe we would meet him again and get some answers. He must understand the importance of Truth.

36. The Meeting of Priests in Constantinople and the Doctrine of Reincarnation

"Now you have seen the most important people and events of the New Testament," said Kualli. "Do you have any more questions before we proceed? We have everything and nothing in our luggage. Did John make clear to you that the free will of human beings rules the world?"

"Unfortunately, yes," I answered. "We have become really thoughtful. We know things that people don't know, and we have no doubts. We are sorry for human beings and for the future that awaits. An awakening is needed."

"The church has not exactly contributed to Truth," said Lydia. "Those who read fantasy come nearer to the Truth."

"Parallel worlds!" I laughed. "Don't I remind you of the Phantom?" I made some silly movements. Kualli and Lydia smiled. Besides that, the atmosphere remained grave.

I went on, "We have not talked very much about reincarnation. In modern times it is almost taboo to talk about it. Was the thought of reincarnation banned at the Nicaea meeting?"

"No. It was banned during the meeting in Constantinople in the sixth century," objected Kualli. "Are you going there, too?"

That was exactly what we wanted. Lydia nodded, I took her hand, and we vanished …

So this was Constantinople! It was a name I had dreamed of many times; it sounded very attractive to me.

We were standing on a terrace and we had a marvelous view of the town and the sea. The dazzling white city looked like a vision, a chimera, in the glaring sunlight. It was so beautiful that I felt a lump in my throat. We came here to find out who caused this act of vandalism, removing the doctrine of reincarnation. This astounding white city did not seem to contain evil, but it certainly did.

At our feet was a very long flight of steps. Thousands of feet must have walked there daily, because it was as slanting and warped as the terrace was even. There was a strong wind blowing, which led us to a street that ended up in an open square. There was a magnificent building where, no doubt, the bishops held their meeting. Lydia approached one of the two guards outside. She said that she was a stranger in town and asked about the building. The guard looked at her sternly and told her that an important synod was going on and that he was there to admit no one but high officials from different countries. Lydia waved at me and sprinkled something on both guards, who immediately fell asleep.

"We are not allowed to do things like that," I whispered, as we hurried through the heavy doorway.

"But we have to," answered my cheerful friend. "Otherwise we can't get inside. Now let's see what the old men are doing." She listened at some doors. While we were standing outside a magnificent doorway, two guards came running towards us.

"We'd better be invisible," whispered Lydia, and I agreed. "Otherwise the old men inside this door will sulk."

After these disrespectful words, we found ourselves in the glamorous sanctuary of the prelates. And the place was crawling with prelates. Although I was monk-dressed, I wouldn't have fitted in with them. They were all wearing very elegant clothes with multi-colored embroidery, not to mention their splendid headgear. They were sitting at a very long table, and their chairs were so abundantly ornamented that there was not even room for a pygmy Angel among the frills. The noise was deafening. At least fifty old men were trying to shout louder than each other. We were standing at either end of the table. We heard a powerful gong sound from somewhere and the noise quieted down. A very small old man who looked bilious stood up. His headgear was half as tall as himself. He banged his fist on the table.

"Transmigration and reincarnation," he shouted." Do we not want to eliminate these ungodly concepts?"

"Yes!" they all cried. It was a "yes" in many different languages, but I didn't doubt it was a "yes."

A tall man in a red cloak, beautifully embroidered with gold, got up and shouted, "In my opinion, everyone who supports the awful doctrine of an earlier existence of souls and the resulting strange belief in the return of the soul to a new life on Earth must be excommunicated!"

There was unanimous consent, but in my ears it seemed more like jabbering jungle-monkeys. The first very small old man rose again and shouted a long question, "Can we all agree upon the following dogmas:

- The doctrine of one simple life on Earth, followed by eternal life in Paradise or Hell.

- The forgiving of sins by the sacrificial death of the Savior.

- Christianity's doctrine of unique divine revelation."

The deafening yell that followed was unbearable. Lydia and I covered our ears with our hands. So, this was Constantinople in the year AD 553: a beautiful city, resting on the seashore, where terrible decisions were made, decisions that would have consequences for the next 2000 years. This was a terrifying thought. Was this really theology? Was this ecumenical? Was this Christian or Cosmic Law?

Rebirth and karma had been given their sentence. Yet they are doctrines that are true for Buddhists. I almost felt sick. For a moment I considered making myself visible and shouting something at this unpleasant parish. Of course, Lydia read my thoughts again and waved her arms to avert me at the other end of the room. I was seething with anger, but I knew I had to control myself. I had to calm down and listen.

A man who seemed younger than the other priests put up his hand and rose. "Who can prove that these dogmas are true? We don't know what happened 500 years ago!" he said, and of course he instantly was booed off.

"We have enough proof from the Meeting of Bishops in Nicaea," the little old man shouted. "They had access to the right gospels. We have to conform with that."

"I have heard that there were hundreds of gospels," protested the young priest. I felt satisfied. Here was a nice young priest who dared to oppose the whole meeting. He continued without taking any notice of the mistrust directed at him.

"I don't believe that humans stay in heaven or hell. There must be other possibilities. The Universe is infinite. I am an astrologer, and I think there are more planets than ours which have some kind of life. I think it is arrogant to make Laws like that."

Now there was a real, unendurable uproar. The young priest was kicked and beaten to the door. His coat was torn to pieces, his face was bleeding, and we saw him fall outside the heavy door, which was slammed shut. We hurried out of the room and went to him. He was lying bloody on the cold stone floor.

Lydia started at once to heal him. I don't know if she used magic, but the young priest came around after a few minutes.

"We are friends," I whispered to him. I was visible now. "We come from the Angelic Realm, and you mustn't be afraid; we're on your side."

"You don't fit in here," added Lydia stroking his forehead. "Find your own parish and keep to it. You are perfectly right; one of the cosmic laws is the rebirth from life to life. But hurry up now and get out of here before somebody finds you. Your life is in jeopardy here."

"My name is Geronimus, and I owe you great gratitude," whispered the young priest. "I will not remain silent about my opinions anymore, and I will find my own parish." He ran out of the building as fast as he could, and we checked that the guards outside were still asleep. Lydia shook her fist at the highly ornamented door.

"Misogynists and blasphemers!" she snarled. "Now we know how the law of reincarnation was wiped out of human consciousness."

"If we go back inside, I cannot keep silent," I promised, and grabbed her around the shoulders. "We have to go home now. The Truth is that the meeting of the bishops was a meeting of traitors, liars, and bullies."

37. The Meeting of Bishops in Nicaea, AD 325

My journeys into the past were indeed so thrilling that I did not want to wake up from them. Anyhow, I was woken up again by somebody shaking me harshly and crying, "Jan, Jan, wake up!"

It was Kualli. I groaned, sat laboriously up, and stared at him.

"Oh, it's you," I muttered. "I have actually experienced things that weren't mentioned in the Bible. I have been in Gaul at the time of Jesus, in what is now called Provence. Since I've never been in Provence before, I really enjoyed the trip. There were beautiful landscapes and interesting people. Because of all these visits, I'm beginning to feel earthly again. Earth seems like a nice place to live, even though people are making trouble here and there. I can now look at the Bible from another perspective. What if my parents had suspected that they were exposed to a real fraud!"

"Just wait and see," laughed Kualli. "You will experience more trouble very soon. We have to scrutinize the fraud that comprises your Christianity even more. Now you are going to Nicaea in the year AD 325."

"The Meeting of Bishops!" I shouted. "Oh dear! Will I partake in it as a bishop?"

"No, just as an observer." Kualli smiled. "You will have your monk's habit on as usual. It is good protection. Lydia will go with you. In Nicaea she'd better stay invisible. Ladies are not welcome at the meeting."

So it happened that I, willingly or unwillingly, was suddenly walking on the uneven paving stones of the small town of Nicaea, situated in Turkey, near Ascania lake. I landed in the middle of a noisy, screaming, and seemingly disordered crowd. There was a wall around the town. I could see some large buildings further on towards the town center. I pushed my way through and heard Lydia puffing at my side. I soon realized that people showed me reverence because of my monk's habit. Some gave way, some nodded in a friendly way and patted me on my shoulder. It is possible that Lydia was patted, too, in undesirable and intimate places, because I heard her snort irritably.

As we got closer to the center of the town, people were more elegant and less riotous. I saw priests everywhere. There were priests of all kinds and of different ranks. Their clothes told us if they were bishops, archbishops, or common preachers. I followed the stream into a big building, probably the High Church where the Meeting of Bishops was to take place. A guard blocked my way at the entrance and pointed to a secluded place for monks. I saw a lot of gray and brown habits crouching down in a corner. The lowest caste of priests, I thought, with an Angel-titter, and Lydia agreed with me.

"Try to get nearer the meeting," she whispered, and I felt her little hand in mine. She dragged me past the monks, who were deep in prayer and didn't seem to react to my pushing and my elbows. At last we had a good view of the meeting behind a pillar quite near the bishops' table. The parish at the table couldn't see me. I supposed Lydia would sit right under their noses and eavesdrop on all they said. She was completely invisible, but I wasn't. I heard some of what was said and I saw them distinctly when I peeped out from behind the pillar.

It seemed to me that the old men did not agree, but they quieted down when a very expensively dressed gentleman came walking in with a lot of courtiers after him. It was Constantine I, and he was seated on a magnificent throne at the head of the table.

The first thing he did was sneeze. I heard a well-known voice in my ear, telling me that she had kissed the emperor on his nose. She giggled when she told me that she couldn't resist. Oh dear, my Angel-friend dared to be so naughty in this place, I thought, surprised. To be invisible is an invitation for mischief, isn't it? I had to warn her and I did.

"If you misuse your task, you can't come with me any more." I said.

"I'm not! Really I'm not!" was her answer, filled with indignation. "I was listening to their talk and I wanted to distract the Emperor, because he highly recommended the bishops to tell fairy-tales in the Bible. They are sitting there making up fables of all sorts. We know the Truth, don't we? It's difficult to be silent. Right now they are talking about the miracles of Jesus. They write them their way, to make people admire and revere. I'm sick of hearing it."

"Are they working on the Bible?" I asked, because now the murmur was very loud.

"Yes, that's the purpose of this meeting. They are creating a fairy-tale. Two scribes are writing down every word they hear. Some old men are disagreeing with everything; it's terrible to hear them."

"Is there anything that makes sense?" I asked. "What's the source of all this?"

"From a gospel. There are at least a hundred gospels. Some priests have devoted themselves to finding old scriptures and taking material from them. That work has been done beforehand. At the moment, John's gospel is under discussion. They are not sure if this gospel is going to be included; there will be a vote about it. Nobody cares if they write the Truth, they are going to create a Bible that makes people scared and obsequious and which gives power to the church."

"They succeeded there," I said grimly. "People at that time needed a common belief that they didn't question for a moment. Please, figure out more, Lydia!"

One after another, the bishops stood up and talked. Sometimes one bilious colleague stood up and contradicted another. The waves of discussion threatened to upset the table many times. Constantine did not talk very much, but when he did, everybody listened attentively. I was almost anesthetized by the smoke from the strong incense and by the glittering of the bishops' clothes. It was nice when Lydia came back and whispered in my ear.

"This meeting will go on for a long time," she panted. "It will last several weeks. The Emperor will only be here for a couple of days to voice his opinions. It seems as if they are constructing a kind of common Christianity, a creed intended for priests and teachers, not for the people. I wonder what may have happened thereafter?"

"Fraud upon fraud," I muttered angrily. A monk sitting nearby cast me an inquiring look. I had to be more discreet.

"Women are being degraded," Lydia whispered, upset. "I wish I dared to give bishop Athanasios a punch on the nose. He is archbishop of Alexandria, and something of a scoundrel. They talk admiringly of Paul, who said that women ought to remain silent in the parish. I think I want to shout!"

I hushed her, and the monk near me looked bewildered. He must have thought I was talking to myself.

My eyes caught sight of a motley crew. Many of the bishops were standing up, looking as if they were going to start fighting. Constantine rapped his staff on the table and there was order again.

"They are constantly arguing about the content of the gospels, if there will be two or four, and who has written them," whispered Lydia. She was silent for a moment, then her voice came back, "Jan, this is crazy! The Emperor says he will let the bishops construct a story, and the most important thing is that people believe in it and that it contains many miracles. He says the church must have the power, and the only way power can reign is through obedience and chastisement."

"Well, I never …" I exclaimed. "Through lies, violence, and compulsion, power has been carried through the ages to this day, where it continues henceforth. Even if the Protestant church has lost its grip today, the Catholic church is still powerful and compelling."

Now the monk near me took alarm. He stared angrily at me, muttered something to another monk, and both of them ran towards the doorway. I ran to the long table of bishops, where one beer-drinking old man after another belched, with his hands on his fat belly. There was not only beer in the goblets, there was certainly wine, too. The air was suffocating.

Suddenly a little devil flew into my head in the middle of the hullabaloo. I swiftly tucked up my cloak and jumped up on the table. Before anyone had the time to say "Jack Robinson," I kicked tankard after tankard into their staring, red, astonished faces. It all happened in an Angelic hurry, but the words that came out of my mouth were not very Angelic. I will not tell you what I said. I got as far as to the other end of the table when Lydia appeared to me. She took my arm and pushed me down from the table before the horror-struck bishops had time to react. It takes time for bishops to react, I happily thought, as I added some mean truths about their blasphemous actions to them.

"Look out, Jan, they've called a guard," Lydia whispered. "We must get out of here."

I felt her invisible hand drag me towards a side door. We didn't get far before we were surrounded by monks and officers of the guard who belonged to Constantine's retinue.

"In the name of the Emperor, monk, you are our prisoner!"

I understood the Latin retort, and to my own surprise I answered him in the same language, "I haven't done anything; I am a foreigner."

I shouldn't have said anything so silly. It was the admission ticket to a cell. The guard who took me there was very brusque. "You will be heard tomorrow," he hissed. "We suspect you are a spy, and spies soon lose their heads in this city!"

It was the last thing I heard, but it was also the last time the guard saw me. I could see his astonished face when I, in an Angelic way, became thinner and thinner and suddenly disappeared. I heard Lydia's happy laughter.

"We cheated that lout!" she tittered. I opened my eyes and saw Kualli sitting on the edge of my bed. His face was rather grim.

"Did you have to go to such extremes?" he asked. "You ought to be punished for interfering in history like that." Then he burst into laughter. "On the other hand, you now know a lot about the church-meeting in Nicaea." He seemed quite content. "You have gotten proof of how false the Bible is. There are only certain clues in it that are true."

"How can I prove that to Bible-believers?" I said dryly. "They will not believe this heretical story. The Bible and the catechism are still important for many people, even if they don't follow the Ten Commandments any longer."

"Only time will tell," said Kualli." The two Jesus prophets, Thomas, Mary Magdalene, and the others who you met are conscious of what happened later. If you are to be able to visit them in their own time and their course of events, they must have contact with you. That is why you are jumping into a kind of repetition of events when you go through these peep-holes. It is difficult for you to understand. Therefore it is also difficult to be convincing. In any case, those who are wise and who seek the Truth understand that the message you bring is the plain and simple Truth."

"But there is another Truth we need to know," I said. "There is something I suspect. Can we visit Jesus in Heliopolis once again? I have a very important question to ask him."

"It's a question that is important for Christianity," Lydia added. She had read my thoughts without my permission. "Come on, Jan!"

"Sit down in the garden by the main building," urged Kualli. "Jesus will come to you. This will be your last Bible journey, Jan!" And he disappeared.

38. Jesus Tells the Truth About His Doctrine

Bougainvillea, camellias, and gardenia grew in thickets, forming a hedge around a stone bench and a stone table. We sat down there. We were visible this time. When I looked at myself I saw, to my surprise, that I was dressed in a long white cloak and Lydia was ravishing in a white, silver-patterned dress. It was a relief to be spared the dull brown monk's habit. We heard birds singing and bumblebees humming, and saw butterflies in lovely colors dancing around our heads. In short, it was absolutely delightful.

Suddenly he was there. Jesus was standing erect and majestic in front of us. He was dressed in a white mantle. He embraced us both and sat down between us on the bench. He seemed more alive than ever. He radiated as much warmth as the Sun, his smile so loving and his grizzled hair reaching far down his shoulders and back. He had a short beard, but no mustache.

Everything seemed to be silent. The bumblebees and the butterflies alighted on flowers and gazed at us. Flowers and bushes that had been swaying in the slight breeze stopped and presented us with their most attractive side.

"What brings you, Jan, and our lovely lady Lydia from the Angelic Realm to visit me again?" the Master asked.

"An idea and a question came to me, which only you can answer," I said. "I have wondered about this for a long time. You have taught your disciples what has been the foundation of your doctrine, even if it has been corrupted since … Master, is it the Buddhism doctrine?"

Jesus laughed. He laughed so heartily and so long that I started to feel uncomfortable. But then he spoke. "At last Truth is dawning upon you, Jan. I was wondering how long it would take. But on one point you are wrong. There are not only facets of Buddhism that I teach, but also some ideas from Hinduism and a lot from the Great White Brotherhood. What I have mostly preached is wisdom from the oldest Indian teachers, from many thousands of years ago. I wandered for a long time in India when I was young, and I resided in the vicinity of many great teachers at that time. They taught me much knowledge and wisdom, for me to distribute as I liked."

"I recognize parts of the Vedas and the Upanishads," I interrupted eagerly.

"Yes. But the most important knowledge has been, and still is, supplied orally from the wisdom teacher to the disciple. It will always be like that – in the future, too. Apart from what has been printed during my time in Palestine, things that everybody understood, nothing has been written down," he told me.

"Do you mean that Christianity consists largely of Oriental teachings?" I asked. "The bishops can't possibly have known about that when they constructed the Bible in Nicaea and Constantinople."

"I have never recommended any new Christianity!" His voice was now very determined and serious. "I feared something like this would occur when I disappeared, but I couldn't do anything about it. I have tried to teach people to be loving and to understand that God 'up there' is the Father of us all and that we are part of Him. I have told you about the Law of Karma and the Law of Rebirth, which are both foundation stones of the Oriental teachings, where what you call Christianity is included."

"Did you learn to walk on water in India?" I interjected.

"Yes, in Tibet, in the far north. You start by sitting on the ground and gradually levitate upwards with the help of your own concentration. In the beginning this is not easy, because you may succeed in levitating four inches and then suddenly fall down if you don't have full attention. It can take many years before you learn to walk on the surface of water. It took me a year. All of the old and wise men in India can walk on water. But this is not wisdom, it is an act of concentration."

"I think it is wisdom to learn to control your body in order to perform this feat," I pointed out. "Can you tell us about other things you have taught that originate from India or Tibet?"

"Oh yes, many things do. I used to say that all life is one before God. Imagine the sea, it is the same sea whether it is still and shiny like a mirror or if the waves are foaming high. It's the same thing with the human soul. It's a part of one single God-consciousness, and at the same time it preserves its individuality. Maybe I didn't explain it with these exact words, but the idea was the same.

"The ancient yogis talked about a little room next to the heart, which is filled with spiritual consciousness. They called the room 'the lotus of the heart.' If you keep that expression in mind, it will be easier to meditate. That's how I started. I became aware that this room existed inside me and I always started from there when I learned something new.

"In the beginning was the Word. The Word was actually OM, or AUM, and that is the most sacred word of Veda. I practiced what you call yoga. It is a hard but useful training. Your thought must become clear and concentrated, because controlled thoughts and feelings have a creative power. It's about uniting the individual self with the highest, all-embracing Self. You unite the subject with the object, the worshipper with the worshipped. Do you understand? If I had not learned the wisdom of the yogi, I would not have been able to preach my faith."

"So you believed in the union with the Highest Self, Nirvana?" I asked. "That is not what you teach, is it?"

"No. I don't believe in Nirvana. You absorb what feels right. I believe in the union with my Father, the Only God. In that union I enter my innermost Self. However, I don't lose myself, like some Buddhists seem to do. Yet I admit without hesitation that I was strongly influenced in many ways by the doctrines I came across in India – not by one doctrine, but all of them. Some ideas from them – quite a lot, actually – became a part of my preaching in Palestine."

"With that, Christianity really comes into a new light," I said, with a triumphant smile. "That is exactly what I've been hoping for when

I want to tell the Truth. It's quite different from what we believe."

"Everyone creates their own Truth," Jesus continued, "and I created mine to reach as many as possible. I succeeded in that, didn't I?"

"Not quite," I answered, and winked to Lydia, who was trying to say something while Jesus and I were talking.

She put her hand up and bellowed, "Can I say something?" She went on without catching her breath. "You talk about God. You often mention His name. At the Last Supper you said, according to the Bible: 'God's name that arouses Love … I have told them thy name and I will proclaim it, because the Love you had for me must be in them and I myself am in them …' What do you mean by that? It didn't come from India or Tibet, did it?"

Of course, a religious historian would quote the Bible, I thought, amused.

Jesus thought for a moment, and then he answered, "Our Father, who art in Heaven, hallowed be thy name … I baptize you in the name of the Father, the Son, and the Holy Ghost … Where two or three are gathered together in my Name, there I am in the midst of them … There, you have three examples of how I used my Father's name. Have you forgotten the Power of Love in the name of God? God's name and Logos, the Word, has a very strong and penetrating power. The Power of Love. That is one of the important laws of my teaching, which you call Christianity. What makes me sad is that I understand that when you last lived on Earth this Christianity involved lots of things that did not come from the Holy Name, not from what I taught. Yet Christ has been added to my name. I never wanted that, because Christ stands for the spark of God, which we all carry within us."

I bent forward and took one of his hands in both of mine. I looked into his eyes and he looked into mine very seriously. "Lydia is right," I said. "How much of it is the East and how much is the Great White Brotherhood?"

Jesus laughed. "I will tell you something," he said, and he looked almost mischievous. "Buddha is one of the Masters of the Great White Brotherhood!"

"What!" I cried. "Buddha is one of them? And you, are you one of them, too?"

Jesus nodded, with a furtive smile. "Quite right. I have used a lot of knowledge from the Eastern teachings," he said. "Much in your Bible is probably from them. You say that the doctrine of reincarnation and the Karma-law are not in the Bible. Well, that knowledge comes from both ways, both the Masters and the teachings. Buddha's name is high on the list of the Ascended Masters. He of course acknowledged the thought of reincarnation, as we all do."

"Maybe things aren't that messy after all," Lydia sighed. "You have given the people a united wisdom, dear Master," she said. "The bishops in Nicaea and Constantinople only chose what would give them supreme power over the people. The rest, which is the most important, they ignored."

"This Bible you talk about must be something modern," objected Jesus. "The original Christianity had its origin far back in time from the Essenes, as I told you before in Gethsemane. It's about time I tell you where the Essenes came from – or are believed to originate. It isn't easy to derive them back in time, but I will try for the sake of Truth. Christianity is really a very modern name for a doctrine that only acknowledged one God and represented the Angelic hierarchy."

"People don't believe in Angels anymore," I interrupted. "Just a few humans believe in us."

"Dear Angel," said Jesus, smiling, "you must make yourself visible more often. But we were discussing the origin of the Essenes. Listen to me: Further back than we can count in years, a remarkable doctrine existed. It was universal in its application and contained eternal wisdom. Actually, some fragments have been found in Sumerian scripts and on stones and bricks that are very old. Do you know how old, Lydia?"

"Yes, 8,000–10,000 years," answered Lydia. "I know, because now we're on home turf."

"Nobody knows how many thousands of years earlier than you say, this doctrine existed," Jesus went on. "Everywhere, in all countries and religions, they have found traces of this doctrine."

Lydia interrupted. "Is that what you call the first Christianity?"

"Exactly," answered Jesus swiftly. "According to my teachers, there is no point in time when it began, but they prophesied how it would be corrupted in the future and be totally changed."

"It can be traced to the mystical Brotherhood who called themselves the Essenes and who lived 2,000–3,000 years before your time," our little religious-historian went on eagerly. "In Palestine and in Syria they were called Essenes and in Egypt Therapeuts. In Egypt they lived on the shores of the lake Mareotis and in Palestine they could be found at the Dead Sea and Jordan.

"We have no earlier names of this Brotherhood. Some believe it comes from the prophet Enoch or from Israel in the time of Moses. You can compare Buddha's holy bodhi-tree to the life-tree of the Essenes.

"Zarathustra preceded the way of life of the Essenes by thousands of years." Lydia loved to talk, and now she was very enthusiastic. "This is something I know a lot about, you see! You can also compare the life-tree to the Tibetan life wheel. I wrote my doctoral thesis about that. Zarathustra or Zoroaster influenced the Brahmans, the Vedas, and the Upanishads, and even the Indian yoga-system. In old Greece, the Pythagoreans and the Stoics followed the same laws as the Essenes. You could also find them in Phoenicia and in the philosophical school in Alexandria. In the West, we find a train of thought from the Essenes in the order of Freemasons, the Gnostics, the Cabala, and a little in Christianity. Jesus, you talked about it in a sublime way in your Sermon on the Mount." She stopped to breathe.

Jesus laughed. "Lydia, I would not have had to prepare my knowledge of history if I had known how fantastic you are," he said. "I only know it up until my lifetime; you can go much further in the future."

"They say," Lydia continued without breaking off, "that the Essenes were very skilled in Chaldean and Persian astronomy and Egyptian healing. They could also predict the future. Some well-known Essenes are Elijah, John the Baptist, John the Beloved, and you, Jesus. Many of their Aramaic texts are in the Vatican in Rome. The Habsburg family in Austria own Essene documents in Slavonic writing, that were saved from Genghis Khan in the fourteenth century …"

"Stop!" cried Jesus, laughing. "Now I lost you. You are in the future. I can understand why you were chosen to come on these trips. You are a walking historical document. But you forgot to say that the Essene greeting has remained the same for thousands of years: 'Peace be with you!' The greeting comes from the time of Moses."

"Oh dear," I sighed, "everything is becoming clearer. I am beginning to understand how everything is connected and how silly these various religions are, and especially Christianity …"

"Christianity is not silly," Lydia protested, "not the old part and not what Jesus preached. It is the prohibitions and fabrications of the bishops that are silly. Don't you agree?"

"Yes," I answered, "but I still find that the Old Testament is only reliable from an historical point of view, and too much of the original teaching is missing in the New Testament. There is no need of a Bible; I think what we need is a Bible-bomb!"

Both Jesus and Lydia laughed. Something else came to my mind: "What about the churches? What will happen to them?"

"I've never seen any church, other than our temples," said Jesus. "They were exploited by the rabbis and used by hawkers and other strays …"

"Churches are the temples of today," explained Lydia. "They were built in connection with the introduction of Christianity. Many of them are gigantic buildings, one more beautiful and noble than another. But one thing they have in common: At the altar you, Master, are hanging on a cross with nails in your hands and feet. Your blood drips and your head droops. I have always hated that image. Why not give people an image of you healing or blessing?"

"Churches could be used for a lot of other things," I proposed excitedly. "You could gather there for meditation or for some important spiritual discourse or even teaching. In our time on Earth, priests could be suitable as conversation-therapists. Some of them could tell stories and fairy-tales of cosmic content for children. We could have festivities there."

"Yes, that's the way it's going to be, if you are to decide," Jesus nodded seriously. "But first I think that Earth has to enter a final stage of evil. So it is said."

"I believe that stage is going on right now," I pointed out, and Lydia nodded.

"Do you have anything more obvious for the readers?" I asked Jesus. "Could any of the old wisdom and knowledge be applicable for people in the twenty-first century? I wonder if knowledge that is more than 8,000 years old can be adapted to a society full of power, violence, pollution, evil, and cruelty? Can the word Christianity have a purer, deeper meaning, away from the boundaries of the Bible?"

"I cannot influence people any longer, since your Bible already has led them astray and provided mendacious information about my lifetime. I would gladly tell you about the laws that were valid originally, much earlier than Atlantis or Lemuria existed on your maps. That is the knowledge that has been passed from human being to human being and which became the basis for Essenes, Therapeuts, and many more. That's the knowledge that in reality ought to have been your Bible and your only guiding principle.

"God created Earth and humans to achieve a positive development. He wanted Earth to blossom and prosper and its inhabitants to live in peace and love. Then he gave people their free will. People used it for destroying and annihilating, not for building."

"Not everything is negative, my dear Jesus," I protested. "The Earth still has so much beauty to offer, so much fruitfulness and righteousness. But we have lost the foundation, which we should stand on. Can you give it back to us?"

"Yes, I can. But it's up to you to utilize it right." Jesus stretched his arms towards the sunny, bright blue heaven in a humble prayer to mediate the Truth.

39. The Foundation of Truth

"Give life the life it was meant to be lived from the beginning," he started. "Forget all the old concepts and see the eternal cosmos tremble during the birth of an unbelievably beautiful Earth. Let the word AUM or OM sound in tune with the Master of Creation and the Creator of Beauty. Let Love flow and gush forth from its own greatness and goodness." For a moment Jesus was silent. Then he sat down between us again.

"God," he said mildly and humbly, "GOD created everything. God is the Power that everything is all about and the ONLY ONE for man to pray to."

"God exists to the full in our time," I added. "In the name of God most wars are fought, in the name of God awful terrorist acts are performed, in the name of God power is transferred to the evil power hunters and in the name of God hatred prospers everywhere. What do you have to say to that?"

"I don't live in your now. I can only regret that God's name has been used wrongly and seems to be totally misunderstood. I wish the old wisdom to be restored and that humans would reconsider. But how can that be done? I mentioned to you before that the world must reach the bottom in order for something new to grow. What do you think?"

"Well, we would like to have a run-down of the basic thoughts of the original 'Christian doctrine,'" I said. "Can you help us with that?" I asked eagerly.

"I will try." The Master had a faraway look, and I felt he was searching deep inside himself to find the right words.

Lydia was on tenterhooks, drumming her foot on the ground. I felt like a calm lake, waiting for the storm.

"GOD!" he exclaimed at last. "God is the content of the first and highest basic idea. You can call this spirit of yin and yang the FORCE, the CREATOR, or FIRST SOURCE if you like. Everything that is contained in this eternal Father-Mother-Energy is the highest guide for man. There is no shortcut. From the God-Power emanates the Sound, AUM. The Sound contains both gentleness and thunder. In the Sound there is Love. God is Love. Love is God. It proclaims the Word, the Sound, the AUM. The word AUM includes the word God. They are One, they belong together, insolubly and eternally. Therefore they are related to the first basic idea. These three are inseparable; they are the Trinity. God, the Word, and Love are the Trinity.

"The Archangels, the Angels, and the Angelic troops come as number two. The Buddhists talk about gods and goddesses. It's the same thing. People are different. They must be allowed to have different opinions about sacred things. The ranking order that is created by man is insignificant. It didn't exist in the beginning. Neither did idolatry. Not going directly to First Source is idolatry. First Source contains All. But the Angelic Realm is full of helpers. They are the followers along the way; they help humans to find and reach First Source.

"Number three is Nature. What is man without Nature? Nature also has direct contact with First Source. Man is a pale reflection of Nature; he is born, lives, dies, and is reborn in the same way as a tree. The Tree of Life is the symbol. Nature contains both plants and animals. Man divides Earth into mineral kingdom, plant kingdom, animal kingdom, and human kingdom. He stops there. For a human, man is the last link in the chain of evolution.

"Nature tries to tell the human that he cannot exist without the four elements: earth, water, air, and fire. The four elements were created first on what you call Earth. The four elements had a long scale of evolutionary phases before man was created. That is why Nature is more important than man and belongs to the first three basic ideas. One day, when man is at last in harmony with Nature instead of destroying it, he will be incorporated into it. The only thing required is to live according to these basic ideas in order for them to be the foundation for a good life. Not many have succeeded with that. Feelings and qualities belong to man. He has not yet learned to manage them. These feelings and qualities are going to ruin the world, but also rebuild it.

"There you have the original wisdom in a nutshell. The Essenes and the Therapeuts have kept and further developed knowledge through thousands of years."

"Can you give us something useful from the Essenes?" I asked.

"Their principles are valid anytime and anywhere," answered Jesus.

Lydia waved her arm. "May I, may I?" she called out. "When I studied the Essenes, I loved their Creed and learned it by heart. I believe it was made much later than the original laws, but few people know about it, and it is really valid for all times. Listen:

1. We believe that our most precious property is Life.
2. We believe that we will use all the powers of life with Love and insight.
3. We believe that mutual understanding leads to mutual connection, that mutual connection leads to Peace, and that Peace is the only possibility for humanity to survive.
4. We believe we must protect instead of waste our natural assets, which are the inheritance of our children.
5. We believe in avoiding poisoning our air, our water, and our earth, which are the basic conditions of life.
6. We believe we will preserve the vegetation of our planet: the simple grass that originated 40 million years ago and the majestic trees that originated 20 million years ago in order to prepare the planet for humanity.
7. We believe it is best to eat fresh, natural, clean, and adequate food without chemicals and artificial manufacturing processes.
8. We believe in living a simple, natural, and creative life utilizing all sources of energy, knowledge, and harmony that exist around us and inside us.
9. We believe that the improvement of life and humanity on our planet must start with individual effort, because everything is dependent on the atoms that create the seed of life.
10. We believe in the Fatherhood of God, the Motherhood of Nature, and the Brotherhood of Humanity."

"I didn't know about this," Jesus said, smiling. "I'm impressed. Something similar was written back in the old times, with different wording. It is a clear account of their goals and meanings, and certainly fits well in your present world."

"Every human being ought to learn these ten Essene commandments, instead of those ten they say come from God. They are obvious antiques."

"The Essenes have a wonderful poem," Lydia added. "I also know that one by heart:

> *I have reached the inner vision,*
> *and through Thy spirit in me*
> *I have heard Thy wondrous secret.*
> *Through Thy mystic insight*
> *Thou has caused a spring of knowledge*
> *to well up within me,*
> *a fountain of power,*
> *pouring forth living waters,*
> *a flood of love*
> *and of all-embracing wisdom*
> *like the splendor of eternal Light."*

(From *The Book of Hymns of the Dead Sea Scrolls*)

Epilogue by Mariana

Perhaps you are now wondering why Jesus didn't accompany Mary Magdalene and his daughter to Gaul and preach his doctrine there? Why did he stay in Heliopolis alone, without meeting his daughter and his wife? He could have visited his son in the Roman Essene monastery. Instead, he stayed isolated in a monastery in Egypt. He taught there for many years, until he went on new journeys in Tibet and India. This is my conclusion, drawn from intensive research.

Maybe Jesus had not the strength to live with his dominating wife. He might have thought they were of better help in different places, than together. Mary Magdalene also gathered people around her. Two prophets in the same place was one too many. Mary was, and is still, looked upon as a woman prophet, especially in France. Perhaps Jesus thought she tried to influence him too much when they lived together. If that was the case, it could have prevented him from continuing the mission that he had come to Earth to perform.

He loved Mary Magdalene, but he preferred to sublimate his love to another plane. Mary grieved for the loss of terrestrial love, in spite of all the love and reverence she got from her pupils and supporters. Sarah hardly knew her father. He thought it was best that way. After the Crucifixion, he was only a tool in the hands of his Divine Father.

I understand if you don't believe this Truth. As Jesus explains: "Everyone has his own Truth." At the same time, I always approve of logic. The Bible is not logical. It is the most illogical book I know. Yet I fully believe that the peep-holes of Jan and Lydia have guided them to true images from the history described in the Bible.

We imagine that people in ancient times were very unlike ourselves. I don't think they were. I really believe that they thought in roughly the same way as you and I. I have used the best sources of history I could find. I had the help of a wonderful, indefatigable librarian, and I learned more about the time I relate here in a short timespan than I did during my whole life. Unfortunately, I hadn't access to the underground library of the Vatican, but other people have already had that. I have also had French and English books and scriptures at my disposal, which gave me much information about the time of Jesus.

I realize that many readers do not accept channeling, but to me it is a very serious gift, even if it is difficult to prove. I have worked with channeling for more than fifty years. Everything must be proven in a scientific way, they say – but what actually is science? I am not from a scientific family. My father was a wholesale dealer and my mother was a housewife. Not until I married a doctor who was also a scientist was I confronted with science. My husband and his friends regarded me as an intellectual mistake. Yet I had left school with excellent marks and had been working for some years as a language teacher.

My husband despised my lack of science. How can you be scientific when you have four kids to bring up? My husband had two children from a former marriage, and together we had two daughters. I started to write when my daughters were small. I wrote two children's books and hoped my husband would be proud of me. He wasn't. I also started to paint. Painting and writing is what I love to do. But there is another thing that broke up my marriage: the occult, the spiritual, the hidden. I was married to an atheist, and with deep regret in my heart I had to make a change.

After the divorce I moved to the countryside, where I still live. I never liked cities; they are not good for a creative mind. I married again, and we bought an old house in the middle of a forest. There I started to write again, and have done that ever since. At last I had time and peace enough to listen to my inner voice. I have always been a psychic, and my second husband encouraged me. My contacts in another dimension helped me write books relating to their reality. And there are many realities!

I have known my friend Jan on "the other side" for many years. It is true that he is a seeker of Truth, despite being in the Angelic Realm now. He is a very well-known, down-to-earth author, loved by many Swedes. When I was looking for Truth, I came across a literature so full of contradictions that I did not know what to believe. Jan has helped me from the first moment he showed himself to me materialized.

It was many years ago, and I was sitting at my desk in front of my computer, starting to write a letter. Then I felt as if someone prevented me from writing and I heard a voice say, "That is not what you are going to write. From now on I will inspire you. You will write books about my journeys on an Angelic level. I am an Angel now. Once upon a time I was a famous writer in Sweden. My name was Jan Fridegård."

Suddenly he stood there, materialized for a very short moment, but I recognized him. I had seen him many times in Stockholm in my youth. He used to be in a bar that I and my friends frequented.

Since that moment he has followed me and inspired me. I am a psychic, and he wanted to continue to write from where he is now. He is a very nice person and he sends his love to everyone who reads this book.

I did not read his books, however, until some years ago. In his last years he was interested in occultism and he wrote a couple of novels that were spiritually influenced.

For Jan and for me, this book reflects Truth. But there is also a true foundation of reality that I found in very ancient scriptures. Nobody can prove if the gospels that have been found are real. They are interesting material and images from old times, when not many people could read and write. That also goes for the time of Jesus. Were the gospels in the Bible really from that time? I don't believe so. Jesus' disciples were mostly fishermen and other craftsmen, and not men who wrote gospels. I cannot imagine any of them writing a diary.

Mary Magdalene and Mary from Bethany are confused in many scriptures and in the Bible, so I have tried to sort that out. Both followed him and both loved him. He was a great man. I have tried to show Jesus, the human being. I wonder how long it takes before people discover how cheated they are. Not to mention the fire-and-brimstone god of the Old Testament. He never existed, because God is Love. This comes from deep inside me, because one night, long ago, I woke up in the middle of the night and heard a loud and distinct voice say, "God is Love." That night was the beginning of a great change in me.

I don't care if I provoke emotional storms in you, negative or positive. I love Life. I believe in a very rich life after death. I believe we will be born into a new and wonderful life in what many call "Heaven" and I call "another Reality." No one can really tell us what will happen; it's a great Adventure. Jesus said, "The Truth will set you free." That's the purpose of this book.

Peace be with you!

Mariana Stjerna

P.S. Greeting from Jan: "If you want to know more, I can make more peep-holes!"

Literature

The Bible, New Testament

The Tibetan Book of the Dead, by W.Y. Evans-Wentz, Oxford 1957

The Gospels of Thomas, Mary Magdalene and Nicodemus (stencils)

The Woman with the Alabaster Jar, by Margaret Starbird, Bear & Co, USA 1993

Marie Madeleine, by Jacqueline Dauxois, Gérard Watelet / Pygmalion, Paris 1998

L'Èvangile de Marie Madeleine, by Daniel Meurois-Givaudon, Editions Le Perséa, Montréal 2000

The Essene letter about the real life of Jesus, by an unknown author. The manuscript was found in Alexandria and the author claims he is contemporary with Jesus and belongs to the Essene Order.

Did Jesus write this book?, by Charles Francis Potter, University Books, New York 1965

Beyond Belief, by Elaine Pagels, Random House, New York 2003

The Gnostic Gospels, by Elaine Pagels, W&W 1979

Jesus Died in Kashmir, by Andreas Faber-Kaiser, London 1977

The Mystical Life of Jesus, by Spencer Lewis, Rosicrucian Order, AMORC 1995

The Essene Gospel of Peace, by Edmond Bordeaux Székely, I.B.S. International

The Teachings of the Essenes, by Edmond Bordeaux Székely, The C.W. Daniel Co. Ltd, London 1977

The Aquarian Gospel of Jesus the Christ, by "Levi"

The Book of the Secrets of Enoch, compiled by R.H. Charles, Oxford and the Clarendon Press, Oxford 1999

Jesus and the Essenes, by Dolores Cannon, Gateway Books, Bath 1992

Bloodline of the Holy Grail, by Laurence Gardner, Element (HarperCollins), London 2002

A Buddhist Bible, published by Dwight Goddard, Beacon Press, Boston 1966